Building and Displaying
Model Aircraft

Robert Schleicher

Building and Displaying

Model Aircraft

Chilton Book Company Radnor, Pennsylvania

Library of Congress Catalog Card No. 80-70385
ISBN 0-8019-6948-4
ISBN 0-8019-6949-2 pb

Designed by William E. Lickfield
Manufactured in the United States of America

1 2 3 4 5 6 7 8 9 0   0 9 8 7 6 5 4 3 2 1

Contents

Building and Displaying Model Aircraft

Chapter 1

Flight

THE re-creation of man's machines in miniature is something more than just a hobby. The miniatures you see on these pages are three-dimensional segments of history. What once was, still is—but in a much-reduced scale. Each of the rivets and lines of the real aircraft has been reproduced on the model by either the manufacturer's toolmakers or by the modelers who assembled the kits. The paint is matched to actual samples of the real paint, in many cases, with subtle touches to duplicate the effects of age and the weather.

These particular kinds of miniature aircraft are far too detailed and fragile to fly. All of the models in this book are made of plastic and not one of the models actually flies. These models are, however, worthy of display in any museum because most of them are so realistic they can almost fool the lens of a camera. When a model is that realistic, it's something more than what most of us consider an ordinary model.

The most astonishing thing about these models is that every one of them was assembled from an easy-to-build kit. Some of the modelers added special parts to alter the kit into another type of aircraft using the conversion process described in Chapter 8. These aircraft look so realistic only because the modelers who built them took the time and trouble to assemble and paint them properly. The quick and easy ways of making museum-quality miniature aircraft from plastic kits have been developed over nearly twenty years of kit-building by hundreds of thousands of modelers. It is their experience that you'll find in these pages. If you learn their secrets, the only missing ingredient will be the time it takes to practice those secrets in building your own miniature aircraft.

The Beauty of Display Models

It is extremely difficult to build a truly accurate scale model aircraft that actually flies—even more difficult than to build such an aircraft in full-size. The difficulty lies in nature herself: you can scale down everything on the aircraft but you cannot reduce the effects of gravity and air density on the model. The miniature aircraft that can fly almost always have

Figure 1-1. Kits, decal markings and reference books allow any modeler to build perfect historical replicas of aircraft, like these two Messerschmitts.

oversize wings and propellors and powerful engines to compensate for the effects of gravity and air density. In addition, it is far easier to damage a miniature aircraft in flight than a full size plane. The pilot sitting in the cockpit of a real plane has both visual and seat-of-the-pants input to help him or her decide when to make a correction that will avert a crash. When you're flying a miniature aircraft, you have very little feeling for the aircraft's movements; most of the control corrections must be made based only on what you can see. There is little point in building a miniature aircraft that is a scale model and then taking the risk of crashing it.

Once you accept those facts, you'll find that there is at least as much satisfaction to be gained from building a display model of a full-size aircraft as there is from building a flying scale model. You can build several dozen plastic models as realistic as those in this book in less time than it takes to build just one flying scale model. Those dozen aircraft miniatures will provide you with many times more satisfaction than that single flying scale model, with no chance that the fruits of your labors will be splattered over a concrete parking lot.

The beauty of most aircraft does not depend on their being in action. In fact, the style and markings that intrigue modelers are best appreciated when the aircraft is stationary. A model aircraft won't look right even in its display "action" setting or diorama unless its detailing is correct.

If you're still not convinced that static or display models of aircraft are just as exciting to build and collect as flying scale models, build one of the larger flying model aircraft in accurate scale. Even if you really love airplanes, you'll find that the amount of time necessary to finish it just isn't enough reward. Most of the master modelers who construct flying scale aircraft also have a collection of plastic display models. The book *Building and Flying Model Aircraft* by James R. Barr and me will give you all the information you need to get started in the companion hobby of flying scale model aircraft. For now, consider the incredible rewards you can obtain duplicating the history of flight with shelf-size model aircraft.

Figure 1-2. The fine painting and decal work makes it difficult to tell the size of the two models from Fig. 1-1.

Figure 1-3. Larry Wright assembled this Airfix 1/72-scale Mirage III and marked it to match an Israeli aircraft from the Six Days' War.

Realism

Realism is what model building is all about. Realism, like beauty, is in the eye of the beholder. The basic premise is the same for most modelers: the miniature should look like the real thing. The difference between one person's model and another's lies in the individual interpretation of realism. There are some modelers, for instance, who feel that a miniature should look as much like the aircraft did when it left the production line as is possible. Others feel that their miniatures will be more realistic if they duplicate the full-size aircraft as it appeared in operation, including the look of wear and tear that results from exposure to the weather or, as modelers call it, "weathering". It requires every bit as much skill to assemble and paint a perfectly realistic off-the-production line miniature as it does to duplicate the effects of weather. Most modelers, however, seem to find it more enjoyable to try to duplicate weathering effects, so you'll see more of those in a model contest than brand-new types.

Implying that a detail is present is often more effective than actually including the detail. The small rivets that are visible on World War II era

Figure 1-4. Just a few of the entrants in a contest sponsored by a local chapter of the International Plastic Modelers Society.

fighters, for example, are so small that they should be almost invisible on a 1/72-scale model aircraft. Yet many kit manufacturers mold in rivets that, if enlarged to life-size, would be the size and shape of half a baseball. The appearance of most 1/72-scale models can be improved if about three-fourths of the rivets are sanded away completely and those that remain are reduced to barely visible outlines. The large gaps that are left around the edges of many removable cowls (engine covers) are another example of the detail itself being less realistic than the mere suggestion of detail. Many 1/48 and 1/32-scale models are actually much more realistic if the removable cowl panels are glued in place so the seams can be filled and scribed to look more like scale-size panel lines.

Remember, every visible detail on the model must be an exact-size reduction of the prototype for the model to appear realistic. If the propellor blades, the radio antennae, or the cockpit "glass" are too thick, then the entire model will look like a toy. A number of modelers spend hours reducing these details to perfection through careful sanding and fitting or by carving new parts from plastic. Some of these modelers neglect the obvious, though, and leave seams between the plastic parts of the model in a size that would be two-inch wide cracks on a real aircraft. The fundamental skill that any modeler must acquire is to assemble the basic kit so the only seams that are visible are those that appeared on the actual aircraft. This technique is covered in the next chapter.

Historical Models

Strictly speaking, any model aircraft you build is an historical model because that model duplicates an aircraft that has already seen action. The most highly prized models in many modeler's collections are miniatures they assembled ten years ago of what were, at the time, "current" aircraft. Today, those ten-year-old models are valuable as historical replicas of the full-size aircraft. The real thing, you see, will have become obsolete through age or modification—it may even have been scrapped. Only the model remains as it was.

Replicas can certainly be created to reproduce aircraft that have disappeared long ago, using only photographs in books and magazines as references for the model. This type of modeling encompasses the skills both of the model maker and of the historian because you must provide the research to insure that your model is, indeed, an accurate historical replica. The shortcut is to simply match the artwork on the box lid. (However, the decals inside are not always as accurate as the lid.) Most aircraft modelers enjoy researching the background of their proposed miniatures at least as much as they enjoy building the model. There is no feeling of accomplishment greater than completing a miniature that precisely duplicates the paint, markings, weathering, and detail of a particular aircraft you have discovered and documented through books and magazines.

Figure 1-5. The two larger aircraft are 1/48 scale, the two medium-size models are 1/72 scale and the one in the center is 1/100 scale in this forced-perspective scene.

When that model is completed, you have actually taken a piece of history and brought it back to life in three dimensions!

Scale Models

The term "scale" describes the proportions of the model as compared to those of the full-size aircraft. Usually, the scale is expressed as a fraction to indicate, for example, that the model is 1/72 the size of the real thing. The best plastic model aircraft kits are precise reductions of the real thing down to the finest detail—even details like the canopy or cockpit frames and Pitot (speed-indicator) tubes are 1/72 the width, length and thickness of those details on the real aircraft.

The term scale has also come to mean that the model is a precise replica. The one-piece plastic toy airplanes sold in department and toy stores may be exact reproductions of the real thing with correct wingspans and fuselage lengths, and even proper shapes. There is no question, though, that they are toys rather than scale models. Some of the pre-painted die cast metal aircraft and Bachmann's type of plastic models are in a vague area somewhere between toys and scale models. These "collector's" models can sometimes be repainted and new decals applied to make them into scale models as realistic as many of those built from kits.

Once you have mastered the techniques in this book, you may want to attempt to make a toy or collector's miniature look like a scale model.

The scale of the model has an obvious effect on the size of that model. You would logically assume that a 1/32-scale model aircraft would be more than twice as large as a 1/72-scale model. That assumption would be correct only if both models (like the P-38 miniatures in figure 1-6) were replicas of similar-size real aircraft. The overall sizes of real aircraft vary tremendously, from "birds" the size of a Piper Super Cub to Boeing 747 jetliners. If the Piper Super Cub and Boeing 747 were both modeled in 1/72 scale, the Cub would be a truly tiny model with about a 5-inch wingspan while the 747 would have a 34-inch wingspan. The concept of "constant scale," where every model in your collection is the same reduction of reality, is charming to contemplate but, as the 747 model illustrates, it's seldom very practical. Most modelers mix several scales in their collections.

The choice of scale for a model kit depends on two factors: how large the model can be and still be practical, and how much detail you want to incorporate. The matter of size is most important, so you seldom see models of four-engined aircraft reproduced much larger than 1/72 scale.

Figure 1-6. Charles Quigley built these P-38 "Lightnings". The smallest one is the Airfix 1/72-scale P-38F, the black one is a Revell 1/32-scale P-38J with a radar dome nose, and the lower left plane is a 1/48-scale Monogram P-38J with Micro Scale decals.

Figure 1-7. If you limit the scale of the models in your collection to a constant proportion you can make comparisons across the years. These are both 1/72 scale miniatures.

Monogram's 1/72-scale model of the B-36 bomber has about the largest wingspan that's practical for a plastic display model: a whopping 38 5/16 inches. You alone must decide how large the models in your collection should be—just remember that you'll have a lot more room to collect models with 10-inch wingspans than models with 36-inch wingspans. Everyone has a few favorite aircraft and you will be tempted to buy the largest kits you can find for those few. When those models are completed, however, you will undoubtedly find even more "favorites" to add to your collection. This type of experience suggests that you should limit your collection to just two or three large ones. Try to buy the smallest-scale kit that has the detail you desire and is acceptable to you.

The need to limit the space for displaying a collection of scale model aircraft has been the primary factor in the popularity of 1/72 scale for plastic model aircraft kits. The average wingspan for a 1/72-scale fighter is about 10 inches so you can arrange a truly extensive collection on a bookshelf. There are 1/72-scale model kits of just about every aircraft that was ever produced, and even a few for prototypes that had production runs of just one plane. The next most popular scale is 1/48; these models are just large enough to allow sliding canopies and interior details but small enough to fit a half-dozen models on a five-foot bookcase shelf. The 1/32-scale models are generally replicas of relatively small fighters but these models still have rather large wingspans, in the 12 to 14-inch range. Nearly all of the 1/32-scale kits feature full engine detail as well as intricate cockpit and landing gear details.

The larger the model, the more detail that can be included without resorting to watchmaker's tricks (like those you'll see later in this book). In addition, the larger the model, the more detail that is needed to make the miniature look like the real thing. Rivets that are nearly invisible on a 1/72-scale model must be included on the surfaces of a 1/32-scale

USAF

Figure 1-8. These Monogram models, a B-52 and a P-51B, are both 1/72 scale. *Photo courtesy Monogram Models.*

model. I have found that most new modelers find it a bit easier to complete a 1/48 or 1/32-scale model to achieve the standards of detail they admire. It takes a bit more practice to build a 1/72-scale model that even appears to have a realism of a 1/48 or 1/32-scale model. A brush mark or a wavering canopy frame line can look extremely crude, for example, on a 1/72-scale model but the same modeling flaws may go unnoticed on a 1/32-scale model. In fact, visible brush marks sometimes match the hurried and crude camouflage paint that was applied on many fighter aircraft during the hectic periods of World War II.

Modeling Kits

Over $200,000,000 worth of plastic model kits are sold in North America each year. Somewhere near half of that figure represents the retail purchases of display model aircraft kits like those on these pages.

Figure 1-9. The full-size versions of this 1/32-scale Corsair F4u1D (left), 1/48-scale P-47D (bottom) and 1/72-scale P-47D (right) are nearly the same size.

Competition in an industry this large has forced nearly all of the manufacturers to produce kits that match the detail and ease of assembly of the best kits on the market. The kits that have been made from steel dies that were cut during the last five years or so are generally far superior to kits produced in earlier years. The earlier kits often included parts that just did not fit together properly and frequently a large amount of the paper-thin "flash," or excess plastic, needed to be trimmed before the parts would fit together at all. Unfortunately, these earlier dies or molds are still being used by a number of manufacturers; you are likely to find a kit made from ten-year-old dies sitting on a dealer's shelf right beside a kit made from newer dies.

It takes years of experience as a model building hobbyist to be able to tell from the box lid which kits are well-detailed and will fit together properly. There are no consumer standards in this area because what one modeler considers poor detail and poor fit may be perfect to another. Besides that, there are dozens of aircraft models that are available only in older kits. In some cases, a kit that produces a model that is not available from any other kit manufacturer may be worth as much as $100 in the plastic kit collectors' market.

If you are a newcomer to this hobby, you should understand that some kits will be very difficult to assemble, requiring a lot of fitting and

Figure 1-10. This 1/72-scale Curtiss-Wright T-32 "Condor" was assembled from a J&L vacuum-formed kit by Jack Stackhouse.

Figure 1-11. Real dirt and Woodland Scenics model railroad foliage were used to create this Pacific Theater/WWII diorama.

seam-filling. If you are having problems assembling what you thought was a simple plastic aircraft kit, you may have one of the models made from older dies. Those older kits will certainly go together once you've developed some of the basic modeling skills. My suggestion would be to put the kit back on your shelf temporarily and buy another aircraft kit. Build three or four kits, in fact, before you attempt once again to assemble that problem model. Other kits that may be hard to assemble are those that are called "snap-together" models on the box lids. These kits will certainly fit together but you may have a rather difficult time filling the seams between the parts. Some parts, like landing gear and propellors, may be so thick that you need to virtually carve replacements for them. Again, if the model looks like it's going to be a real problem to complete, set it aside and try a few others.

The vast majority of the plastic model aircraft kits on the market fit together precisely, with very little of that excess plastic flash, and most have perfect scale detail. These models require only a touch of filler to hide the seams and there's little point in trying to improve on the detail because what's there is right. You should be aware of the exceptions to this rule so you'll know that it's not just you; there truly are a few kits that are far more difficult to build than it would seem from a casual glance at the pieces. It is difficult to list the bad ones for two reasons: First, what I consider to be an assembly problem might be easy for you because you have some other hobby or work experience. Second, a kit that might be a problem today may be repackaged with (or without) reworked production dies. Once you have assembled a few kits using the seam-filling, painting, decaling, and detailing methods in this book, you'll find that there is no such thing as an impossible-to-assemble kit—there are only kits that might challenge an experienced modeler.

Pleasures of the Hobby

The assembly of display model plastic aircraft can be as far removed from toy planes as you want to make it. The only aspect of the hobby that is shared by everyone is the completed models themselves. For some, the hobby consists of quickly assembling as many models as possible in an attempt to build a large and complete collection. For others, the research for a single kit's paint and decals may consume a month or more of spare time. Some of the modelers that take the time to research special markings and paint schemes for their kits don't bother to try to make the model

Figure 1-12. If you'd rather "fly" your models than look at them, they can be used to play three-dimensional war games. The clothespin and pole are part of the playing pieces for this game. *Photo Courtesy McEwan Miniatures.*

look like a showpiece—they simply want something different. Still others spend several weeks researching their model and a few more weeks assembling the kit, painting it and applying markings and decals so it is a museum-quality replica. Some modelers add scale-model landing fields or portions of aircraft carrier deck to their display areas to create miniature dioramas. There is even a growing percentage of aircraft modelers who use 1/144, 1/100 or 1/72-scale models to fight mock dogfights in three-dimensional war game simulations.

You'll find all the information you need in this book to develop your skills in any or all of these areas of the hobby. There is more to the model aircraft hobby than gluing pieces of plastic together. In one way or another, the techniques you'll see here will help to bring the entire world of aviation to your fingertips.

Chapter 2

Kit Assembly

THERE is a lot more to assembling a plastic model aircraft kit than simply reading the instructions and gluing the parts together. The pre-colored plastic parts, decals, and words on the box like "Easy-Assemble" or "Snap-Together" may give you the impression that the box is right and this kit is truly suitable for "Ages 8 and Up." You may have already discovered that those plastic parts assemble into nothing more than a plastic toy; a well-detailed toy, to be sure, but one that bears little resemblance to a real airplane. The problems with these kits are easy enough to see: unpainted plastic looks like plastic no matter what color is molded into it, and the seams between the parts of a model are many times wider than the seams between the panels of a real aircraft. The miniatures you see on these pages look like real aircraft for two basic reasons: they appear to be a single unit rather than a collection of plastic parts, and they have been painted and marked with decals so the finished surface looks as smooth and solid as any full-size aircraft. The plastic used for model kits has a translucent appearance that can only be disguised with paint. Paint will not hide the seams between plastic parts, however, so that unified appearance begins with the assembly of the kit's pieces.

The Workshop

It is possible to assemble a plastic model aircraft on a breadboard while you're propped up in bed. When it comes time to paint the model, however, you'll have to make arrangements for some additional work space. Don't use the lack of a permanent workshop as an excuse to delay building models or, worse, as a reason for assembling them now and painting them later. I really don't know of a single modeler, either amateur or professional, who is completely satisfied with any model he has ever completed. All the experts do just what you should: they strive to make the next model better than the last.

The cements and paints used in building plastic models are all flammable and most are toxic. Inhaling or swallowing them will make you very sick, at the least. The area you set aside for your workshop, then, must have adequate ventilation by means of a partially open window or a fan. The kitchen is perhaps the worst possible place to build plastic models because of the danger of pilot lights, ovens and other sources of fire. There is also the chance that you could contaminate food with your cement spills or paint fumes. A service porch or laundry room will be suitable only if there is no gas heater or clothes dryer that might have a pilot light or other flame. The best way around the problem is to install a small window fan or an inexpensive furnace vent hood and fan placed on its edge in front of an open window. The goal is to position the fan so that all the cement and paint fumes are pulled out the window and into the open air, well away from any open flame. If you cannot work directly in front of the window, put the fan on the workbench and direct its exhaust into a flexible plastic hose sold for clothes dryer vents. Lead the hose to the window.

The other important requirement for any workshop area is adequate lighting. Room light is seldom bright enough for you to see exactly where the cement is flowing, or whether a decal is applied properly. Supplement the room light with two table lamps or a double-bulb fluorescent light. The two lights are necessary so you don't find yourself working in your own shadow. There are enough portable lamps that have flexible necks or adjustable reflectors to fill a book. Do try to buy a couple that can remain in the workshop so you don't have to borrow one from some other area of the house whenever you work.

Tools for the Modeler

If you have proper ventilation and adequate lighting, you can assemble most aircraft kits with nothing more than a sturdy work surface, a pair of tweezers, a hobby knife, and liquid cement for plastics. Any additional tools that might make your work a bit easier will be described when their use might be appropriate. The set of handtools in figure 2-1 will make it easier to add superdetails like cockpit interiors, "down" wing flaps and the like. The entire set of tools should cost less than $50.

There is one relatively expensive tool that is recommended: an airbrush with an air compressor and an air pressure control valve and gauge. The single-action airbrushes that mix paint internally are just fine and they generally don't cost more than $35 to $40. The air compressor can be as small as 1/12 horsepower, but it will run in the $50 to $150 range with its air pressure gauge and valve. If you live in a humid climate, you'll also need a moisture trap which will run another $20 to $30. Most modelers believe it is worth the $100 to $200 for the airbrush rig but you'll have to make that decision for yourself. It certainly is possible to paint and even weather plastic model aircraft using nothing more than spray cans of paint and paintbrushes. But you will get much better results if you can apply the paint with a scale-size spray.

Preparing for Assembly

The actual kit assembly should really begin when you open the box. Carefully remove the instructions and be certain you have left all the parts and decals in the box. Next, read the instructions from beginning to

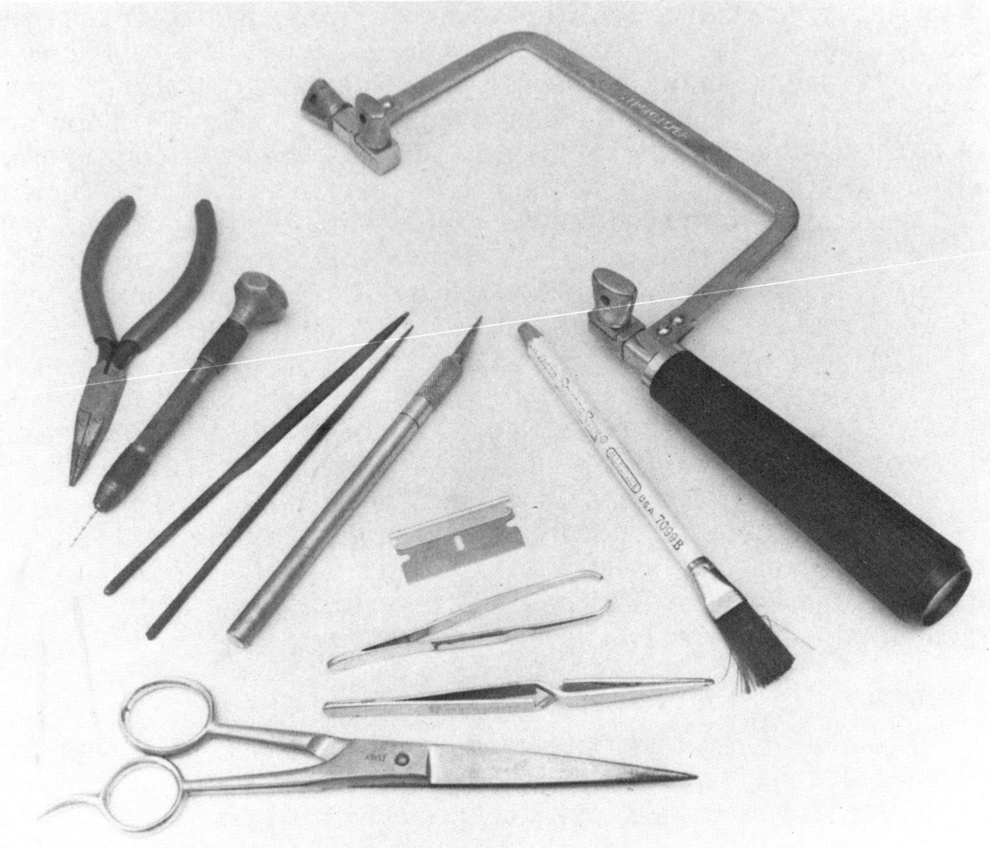

Figure 2-1. The basic tools are (left to right): needle-nosed pliers, pin vise with drill bits, flat and round jeweler's files, hobby knife with blades, single-edge razor blade, spring-open tweezers, self-clamping tweezers, scissors, typewriter eraser, and jeweler's saw.

end—don't skip a word. Read through the instructions a second time while you examine each part with all the parts still attached to the molding sprue or tree. This step will give you a chance to determine just how much of the plastic is usable and how much is scrap plastic molding sprue. You'll also be able to tell the difference between excess plastic flash and alignment pins or rivets. The flash is the plastic that squeezes out from between the halves of the steel die or mold that formed the part at the kit manufacturer's factory. If you cannot tell for certain what is part and what is flash, leave the "extra" plastic until the model is partially assembled and you can see how the piece looks when it is really part of an airplane. Sometimes only an expert in the details and appearance of the full-size aircraft can tell which of those little wisps and blobs are details and which ones are scrap plastic.

As the next step, most modelers trim all of the parts from their sprues so the parts can be test-fitted together in a run-through of the instructions. There are those who prefer to leave the smaller parts on the sprues so the sprue itself can serve as a handle until the part is painted. Try both methods with several kits until you find the one that works best for you.

Most plastic model aircraft kits are designed so they can be assembled without any tools—the parts could be broken from their molding sprues or trees and glued into the alignment holes with a tube of plastic cement. That is the wrong way to do it. Never, ever, break a part from its molding sprue or tree—you might leave a large portion of the part behind. Always use a hobby knife to carefully cut the part from the plastic sprue or molding tree. Even if the part still breaks off the molding sprue, you will control precisely where it breaks with the pressure from the knife blade. Once it is cut, clean up the place on the part where it was attached to the sprue with a jeweler's file or shave it smooth with the hobby knife.

Notice that you have not actually assembled anything yet but, if you're wise, you have gone over the instructions at least three times.

Fitting the Parts Together

The term "fit" is relative when it comes to plastic kits. Frankly, there isn't a kit on the market that doesn't have one or two parts that need to be trimmed slightly at their attachment points for a perfect fit. The long seams where fuselage halves meet or where the tops and bottoms of wings join must fit snugly together. You may need to file or scrape a bit of plastic from the joining surfaces. You may even find that some of the aligning pins actually don't align the parts, as shown in figure 2-2. The best cure for misaligned pins is to simply slice off the pin with a hobby knife. Pay particular attention to the way internal parts like cockpit floors and engines fit. Often, these parts don't line up with their own alignment tabs, making

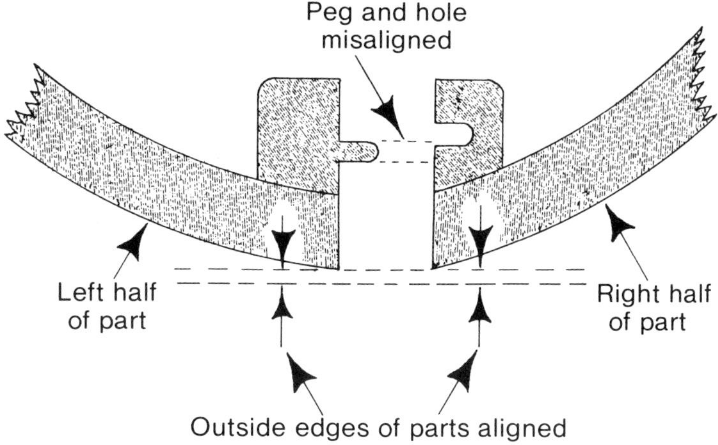

Figure 2-2. Cross-sectional view of ill-fitting fuselage alignment pin.

it impossible to fit the fuselage halves together tightly. This is the type of misfit that you should discover when you go through that dry run with the instruction sheet and the parts. If the parts you are assembling are plated, the plating must be scraped from any areas that will be glued together. Plastic cement works with a solvent action so it must only be used on bare plastic surfaces.

There are two methods of removing just a trace of plastic to obtain a perfect fit between the parts. First, the adjoining surfaces can be filed lightly with fine-toothed jeweler's files. The jeweler's files are available in a dozen different shapes from most hobby shops. The square, flat, and round files are best-suited for plastic aircraft. Buy medium to fine-size teeth if you have a choice. The other method is to scrape or adze the surfaces with a hobby knife. Adzing is a term derived from the early woodworkers who used the pulling motion of a special adzing tool to shape and smooth wood surfaces. To do the work with a hobby knife, hold the blade as

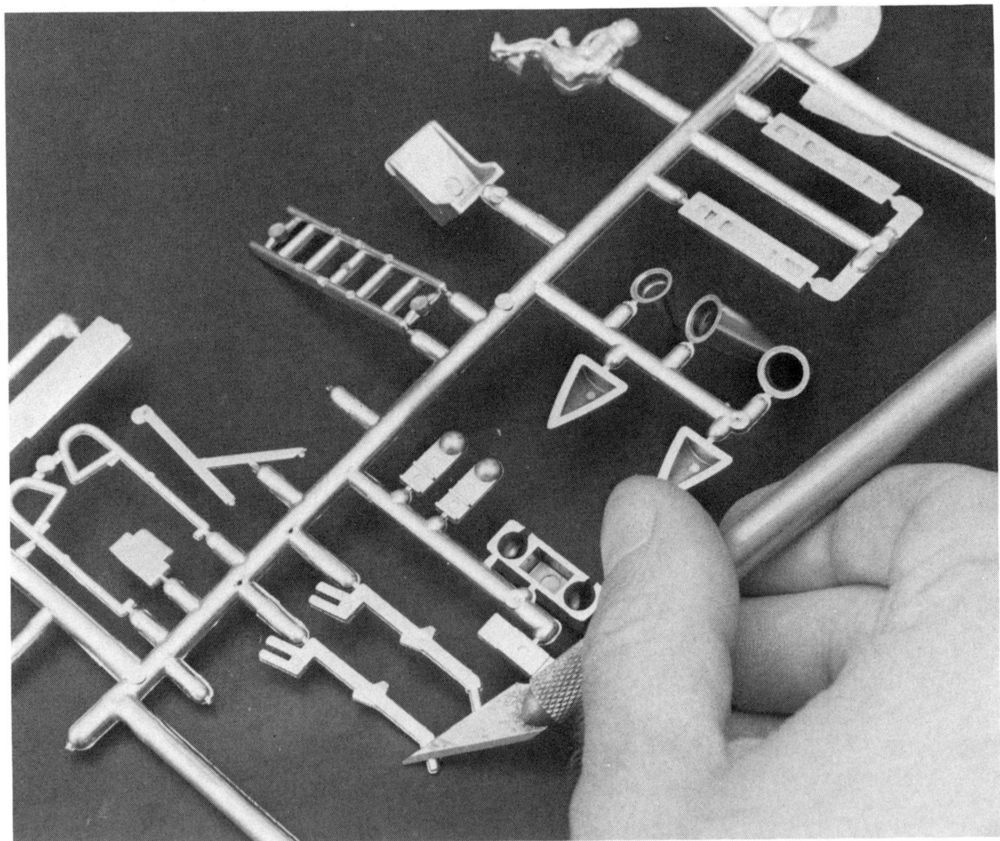

Figure 2-3. If parts are plated, the plating must be scraped from any joints to be glued.

though you were going to shave a sliver of plastic but pull the knife lightly so the blade trails and scrapes rather than cuts. It takes just a little downward pressure to make it work and only a few shavings or sawdustlike particles of plastic should be visible. This technique is used to remove just a few thousandths of an inch of material at a time.

Glues and Cements

You must use two different types of cement for plastics to build any model aircraft kit: the type in a tube and that in a bottle. Cement from a tube should be used on fuselage and wing seams where there is an extremely long and thin glue joint. The bottled liquid cements for plastics are the best choice for virtually every other plastic-to-plastic joint on the model. The tube cement includes a dissolved thickening agent that can delay the drying time for as long as a year! The joint will appear to be dry and hard but, after paint is applied, the glue seam will continue to shrink or depress for months. The only ways to avoid the problem are to use as little tube cement as possible and to use the liquid cement for most joints.

There are at least a half-dozen different brands of both tube and liquid cement for plastics. I strongly recommend that you purchase at least three different brands of each type of cement. Different brands react in different ways under specific temperature and humidity conditions. I have found, for example, that Micro Scale's Micro Bond tube cement is much thinner than Testor's tube cement but that the Micro Bond dries too rapidly for really long seams on, for example, a 1/72-scale bomber. I have also found that the Plastruct brand Plastic Weld liquid cement is a bit thicker than Testor's Liquid Cement for Plastics. Some modelers use a thicker cement, like the Plastruct, for small joints like landing gears, where a quick and secure bond is needed. Testor's liquid cement is most useful where large areas, like two wing halves, are to be joined.

A word of caution: do not, ever, try to use either tube or liquid cement to fix an ill-fitting joint. An excess amount of either type of cement will hold the part in place but that years-to-dry delay is virtually guaranteed. If you cannot make a small shim of plastic to wedge the part in place, use five-minute or regular epoxy cement for that particular problem joint. If you are merely concerned with an unsightly gap or seam, use regular plastic cement and, after the cement dries, simply fill in the gap or seam with putty as described later in this chapter. Another warning: do not use a hot knife (a type of woodburning pencil with a knife tip) or flame near any joint that has been cemented—the heat can combine with the residue from the cement to form highly toxic gases!

Liquid Cements   All of the liquid cements for plastics look like water, smell like solvent, and work by literally melting or dissolving the plastic. The dissolved plastic eventually dries as the liquid cement's solvent evaporates. The resulting joint is virtually welded in plastic. The joint will usually be just a bit weaker than solid plastic because the solvent leaves microscopic holes or cavities as it evaporates.

The liquid cements flow almost like water which means you can take advantage of some of the properties of a liquid to make the cement go just where you want it. If, for example, you are holding two halves of a stabilizer together with your fingers or clothespins, you can just touch the seam between the parts with a paintbrush full of liquid cement. Capillary action will force the cement to flow along the seam. It may require several applications, to different places on the edges of the seam, to get the liquid cement spread all the way around the part. The point here is that you don't apply liquid cement to the parts before you assemble them as you must with tube cement. However, you may pre-coat the mating surfaces with liquid cement to partially soften the surfaces so they will more readily accept the later outside application of liquid cement. This technique is only effective on seams that are between two and four inches in length because longer seams allow too much time for the cement to dry before assembly. You can use either a small (number 0) paintbrush or one of the adjustable (with a knurled knob) drafting pens to apply the liquid cement.

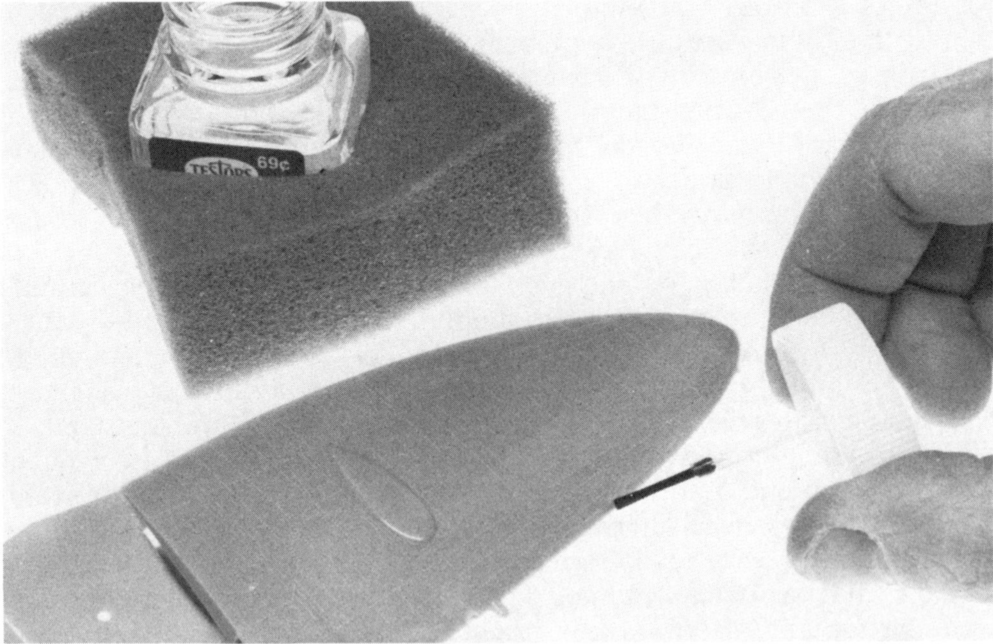

Figure 2-4. If the parts fit together properly, you only need to use liquid cement for plastics. The foam helps to keep the bottle from being knocked over accidentally.

Applying Cement

With practice, you can make a line of tube cement as thin as a straight pin just 1/32 inch from the outer edges of the plastic part. If you get too much cement in the area, wipe off the excess with a toothpick. Work quickly so the cement won't dry before you can put the fuselage or wing halves together. When the two halves are mated firmly together, run a coating of liquid cement all around the seam to partially dissolve any of the tube cement that dried too rapidly and immediately squeeze the parts together a bit tighter. If the parts are not warped and if you have carefully fitted the joints, you should not need any type of clamping devices.

Most of the larger plastic parts, like fuselages and wings, will warp a small amount after the plastic cools from the molding process. If these parts are warped, you must devise some type of clamping arrangement to hold them together for at least 48 hours after the glue is applied to the seams. Try to clamp the parts together with clothespins at the thinner areas and rubber bands for the thicker areas as shown in figure 2-6. The clamps must not touch the joint or the glue will be attracted to the clamps themselves, and will ruin the exterior surfaces by gluing the clamps to the model in dissolved plastic. The clothespins can probably be arranged so they don't touch any glue seams. A pair of toothpicks, on each side of the glue joints, should raise the rubber bands clear of the joint until the glue dries. Do not let the toothpicks touch the glue. Test-fit your clothespins

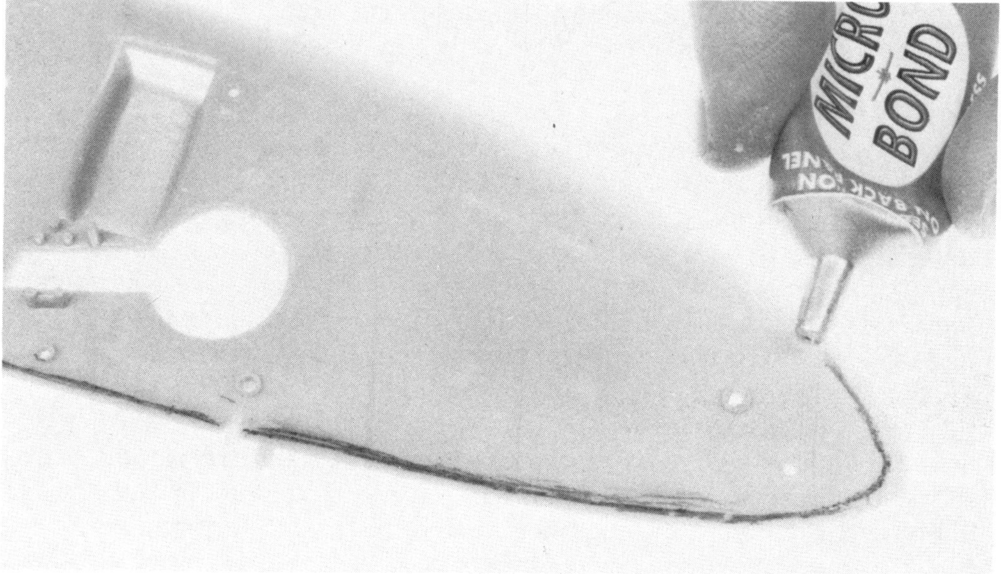

Figure 2-5. The blackened line indicates the area, just 1/32-inch from the outer edges, where a thin bead of tube cement can be applied to joint wing or fuselage halves.

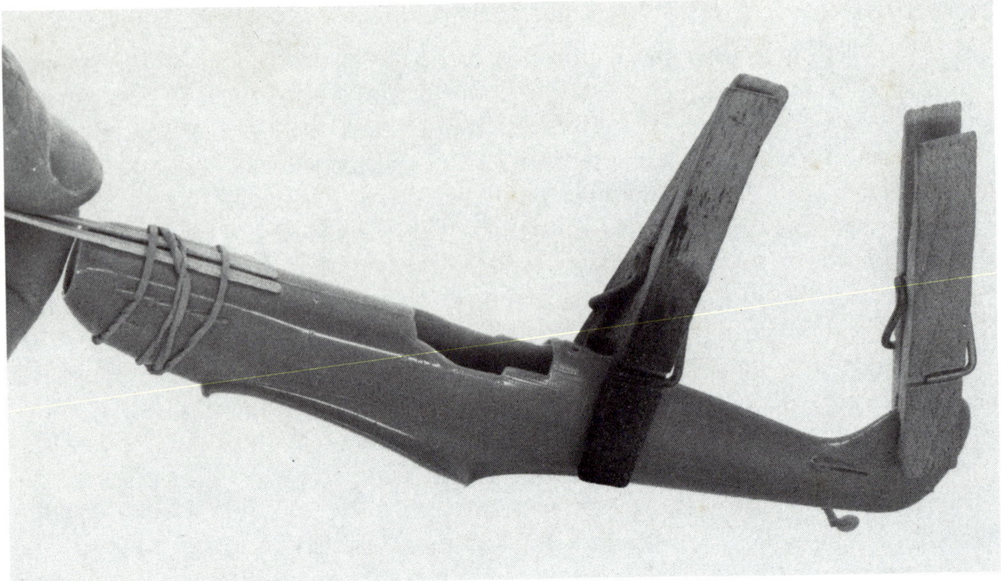

Figure 2-6. Use clothespins or rubber bands with wooden toothpicks to hold parts that are warped.

and rubber bands *before* you apply any glue. Apply the tube cement to the fuselage or wing and press the two parts together, then apply the clothespins and rubber bands (don't forget the toothpicks on each side of the seams). The liquid cement for plastics can now be applied and the parts squeezed together a bit tighter with your fingers.

Filling the Seams

The most important lesson you can learn from this entire book is that you must try to disguise *every* seam between the parts of a model. There is nothing that detracts more from the realistic appearance of a plastic model aircraft than the unsightly cracks that would never exist on a real aircraft. It will take some practice and the building of several models before you will be able to tell whether a seam will be visible *after* the model is painted. Don't worry too much, though, because you can apply most types of filler putty after the model is painted and just touch up the areas that have been filled.

Obviously, it's a lot easier and cleaner to find the cracks and seams before you paint. If you went back over the seams with liquid cement and squeezed the parts tightly together with your fingers, as suggested, you should have forced some of the cement-dissolved plastic out of the seam to form a very thin bead of plastic all the way along the seam. This bead of plastic may have done almost all your seam-filling for you. With practice, you'll learn just how much liquid cement and how much finger pressure is needed to make a bead that will almost completely hide most seams. The trick is to use just enough cement to form a hairline bead of plastic but not so much as to cause those depressions that occur over a long time. When the cement has dried for at least 48 hours, you can use a hobby knife to carefully shave that thin bead of hardened plastic flush with the surface of the model. If you do this carefully, you may even be able to trim the glue bead without shaving away any of the molded rivet or panel details that are near the seam.

There will be some joints between parts of the model where you cannot use the cement-and-plastic bead trick to hide the seam. The areas where the wings and stabilizer join the fuselage are examples of places where only a minimum amount of cement can be used without the danger of creating a cement sink. Those areas (and any areas where the cement-and-plastic bead trick did not work) must be filled with putty. I have found three types of putty that work successfully: the relatively thick automobile body shop's "Spot Putty," the somewhat thinner Duratite brand White Model Putty, and the very thin Micro Scale Quick Silver putty. Do not use a layer more than about 1/32 inch thick of any of these putties, or their solvents might melt or sink the plastic. If you need to build up an area thicker than 1/32 inch, just apply several 1/32 inch coats of the putty. Again, I would recommend that you purchase all three types of putty if you can find them. You may find that one brand works better than others in your particular climate or with your particular modeling techniques.

The technique used to apply putty is the same for all of these brands. Use a flat toothpick to spread a layer of the putty over the seam so the seam is completely buried in the putty. Apply about 1/32 inch more putty than you need so there is extra putty to sand and shape to match the contours of the surrounding areas. Let the putty dry overnight, then sand it flush with the surrounding surfaces using 400-grit sandpaper or emery paper wrapped tightly around a wood tongue depressor or ice cream stick. Wrap the sandpaper around a paintbrush handle to sand concave areas. Work slowly and carefully so the putty blends in with the surface of the model. You will undoubtedly sand off some of the rivets and body seams when you use any of the filler putties. However, the missing surface details will be far less noticeable than that horrible gap would have been. If you wish to replace the details, you can simply scribe in the panel lines with a sharp hobby knife. The technique for making rivets with a straight pin is described in Chapter 7.

Special Glues and Cement

Never attempt to install a clear plastic canopy, cockpit, gun blister or any other clear or translucent plastic part with *any* type of plastic cement. The solvents in plastic cements will fog or craze the clear plastic parts. You can use five-minute epoxy to hold any parts you are reasonably certain

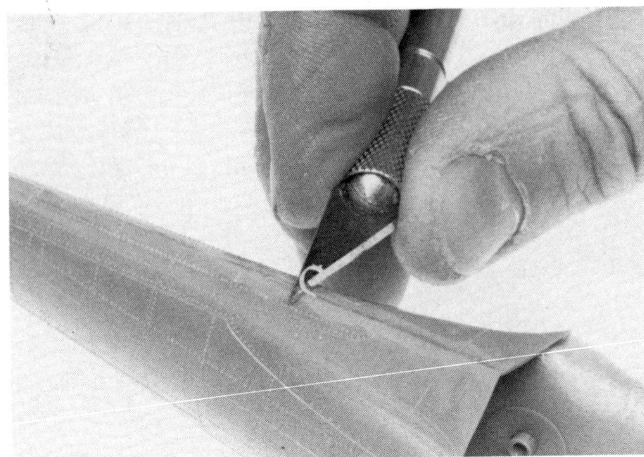

Figure 2-7. Carefully slice the glue-and-plastic bead from the edges of the seams after the glue has dried for 48 hours.

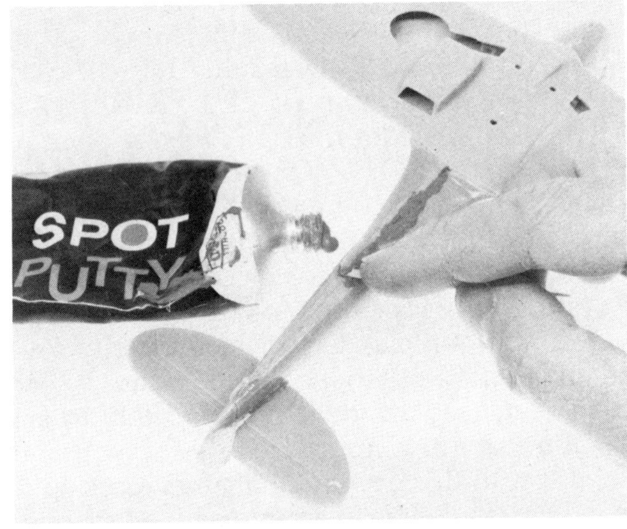

Figure 2-8. Spread a thin layer of filler putty over all of the seams with a wooden tooth-pick.

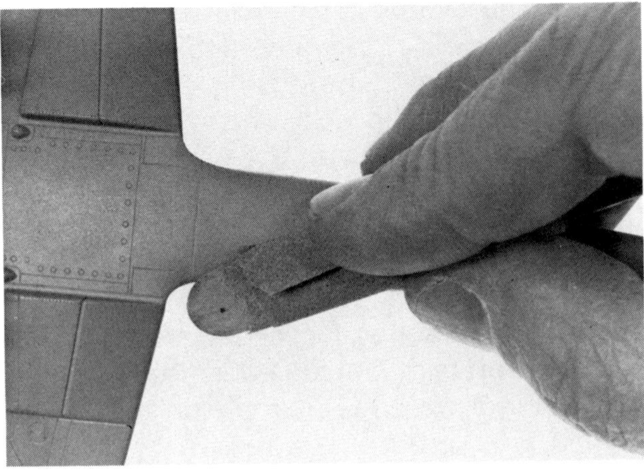

Figure 2-9. Wrap fine-grit sand-paper over an ice cream stick when you sand the filler putty flush with the surface of the model.

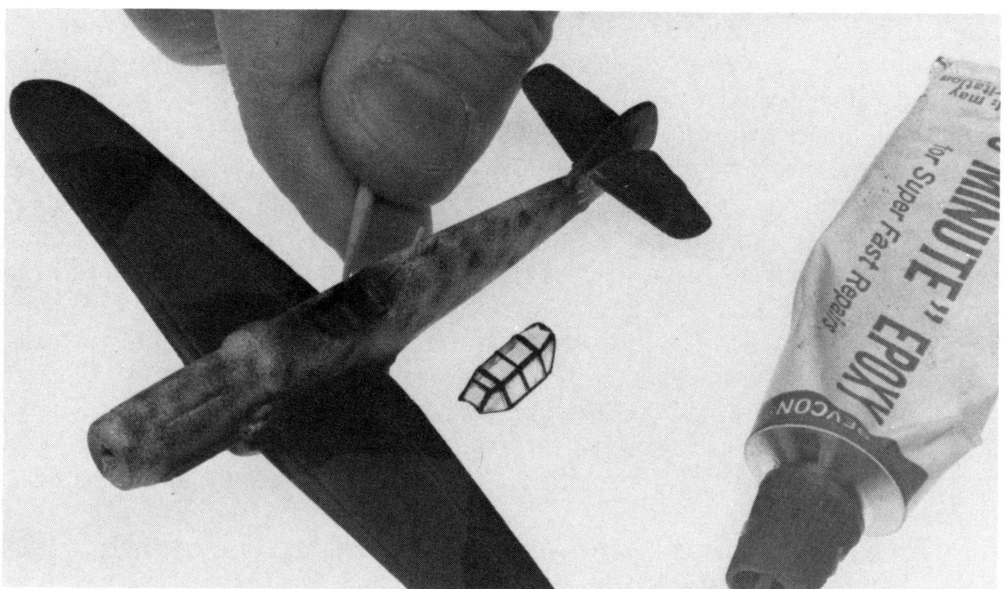

Figure 2-10. Five-minute epoxy or white glue won't etch the clear plastic of canopies.

Figure 2-11. Five-minute epoxy is much better than plastic cement for gluing joints that must be strong, like landing gear and wheel-mounts.

you will never remove again. If you feel you might want to remove the part someday, to install a pilot or add cockpit detail, then glue the part in place with common white glue. The epoxy or the white glue will hold the plastic firmly without any chance of fogging or etching. The five-minute epoxy is also the best choice for very small joints where high strength is needed. You can attach the landing gear, tail wheels, radio and radar antennae, guns, Pitot tubes, and landing gear flaps with five-minute epoxy.

Some modelers are experimenting with the use of the various types of cyanoacrylate cements like Eastman 910, Zap, Hot Stuff, Krazy Glue and the like to assemble their plastic models. This stuff is tricky because it flows like water but will stick to your fingers more readily than to plastic. If you want to try it, use one of the thicker types like Goldberg's Super Jet. The cyanoacrylate cements require a very tight-fitting joint but Super Jet contains a thickening agent that acts as a built-in seam filler for smaller seams.

To fill small seams with cyanoacrylate cement, first sprinkle some baking soda into the seam and shape it with a toothpick to serve as a seam-filler or putty. Add a drop of the thin cyanoacrylate cement and the baking soda will be harder than most putties.

Cement Solvents

One of the problems in working with cement is that it always finds its way onto your fingers and then onto the model's detail surfaces. You can minimize the problem by minimizing the amount of cement you use.

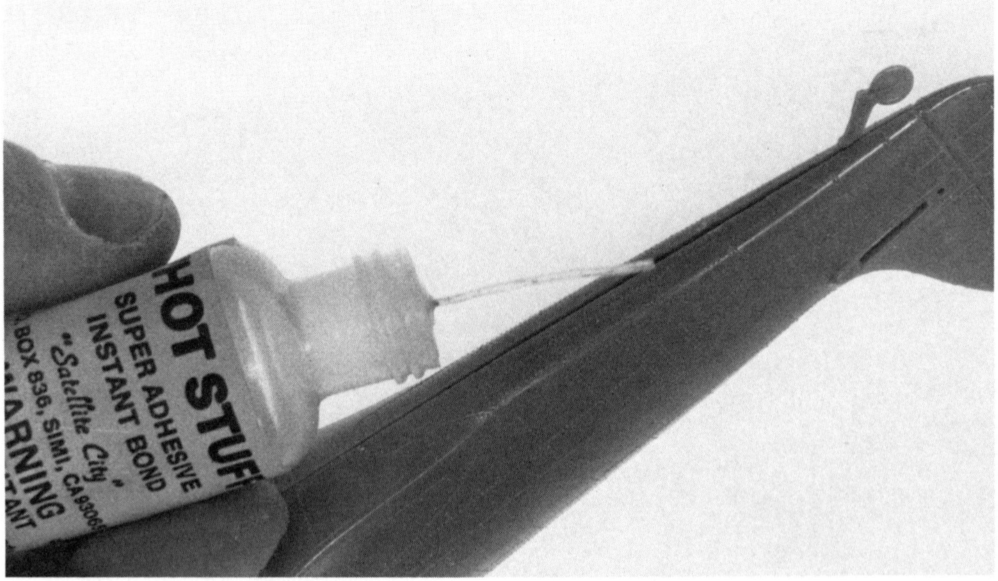

Figure 2-12. Some modelers prefer to use cyanoacrylate cement to assemble their plastic model kits. This requires extra skill.

If you do get it on your hands, you should have a remover readily available so you can keep your fingers clean. Acetone will remove almost any of the plastic cements or putties. Acetone is the principal ingredient in most fingernail polish removing fluids so you may already have some in the house.

There are now some special pastelike fluids (Duro's Super Glue Remover is one) that will help to slowly dissolve the cyanoacrylate cements from your skin. The removal of the cyanoacrylates is still a problem and it can be painful even with the removers because you often have glued skin to skin! So far, I know of nothing that has been developed that will remove epoxy and not take skin with it. If you only have the resin *or* the catalyst on your hands, or if you can catch the problem before the epoxy cures or hardens, you should be able to wipe it away with a rag and some lacquer thinner.

Chapter 3

Painting with Brushes and Aerosol Cans

THE hobby of building miniature aircraft from plastic kits is really the hobby of *painting* miniature aircraft. It does take some skill to assemble a model with filled seams and neat glue joints, but you'll perfect those techniques after building a few models the right way. If you truly prefer building to painting, you may enjoy working with conversions to modify exisiting kits or you might concentrate your efforts on the vacuum-formed kits. Most of us, though, discover that the painting of the model and the research that makes the painting a perfect historical simulation are the real core of the hobby.

A perfect paint job cannot hide a kit that has not been assembled properly. In fact, the proper methods of paint application are designed to accent details and those "details" could well include poor glue joints or partially-filled seams. You may be surprised to learn that your own eyes can distinguish the difference between a coat of paint that is too thick and one that is almost a perfect scale thickness. This difference may be as little as .002 inch but that extra thickness is quite visible over rivet or seam details.

The real secret to a perfect miniature aircraft is to cover a properly assembled model with the thinnest possible layer of paint. The color coats of paint will be covered with an initial coat of clear paint, the decals, and a final coat of clear paint to protect the decals. Fortunately, the clear paint does not hide the details as much as the color paint does.

Paints

The choice of paint for your model begins with the full-size aircraft. You'll want to select colors that match that aircraft and find a means of applying them to match the patterns on the prototype. If you are going to apply the paint with a brush or with aerosol cans, you should be extremely careful about which paint scheme you select for your model. There are almost always two or three variations of color schemes on full-size aircraft and there may be hundreds of variations. Some of those paint schemes are almost impossible to duplicate with a paintbrush or with spray cans. Save the troublesome paint schemes for future models. It is virtually impossible, for example, to duplicate the appearance of unpainted aluminum using either a brush or aerosol cans. Testors makes a few kits for aluminum aircraft in which the plastic itself is plated. These kits can be quite realistic when they are properly weathered but that, too, takes some practice. Try to find a photograph of the full-size aircraft with a feasible paint scheme.

The second type of paint scheme that beginners should avoid is one with a shaded or blended color separation line. The only truly successful way to duplicate these types of finishes is with an airbrush like those in the next chapter. You can try to simulate the shaded color separation lines using the techniques in this chapter but only an airbrush can duplicate the feathery edge between the colors. If you can find a prototype for your model that has sharp color separation lines with no bare aluminum areas, you can duplicate that finish just as effectively with a paintbrush or aerosol cans as you could with an airbrush. The trick is to find photos of the real aircraft and decals that allow you to duplicate its markings as well as its colors.

There are a limited number of paints suitable for model aircraft that can be applied in the thin coat that you need. Avoid *any* brand of gloss finish paint. The gloss is essentially clear paint with the color pigment mixed in. It takes a very, very thick coat of gloss color to hide the plastic. You should also avoid any paints that are not intended for plastics unless you can apply them with an airbrush. Floquil's standard line of paint (they also make water-soluble Polly S paints) will etch or craze most plastic model aircraft surfaces unless a coat of Floquil's Barrier liquid is brushed over the model. Unfortunately, the Barrier is a relatively thick paint that, in my opinion, defeats the purpose of using Floquil to achieve a thin color coat.

The best paints for use with a brush are the water-soluble Polly S series, the Scalecoat II series of paints, or the flat finish enamel paints by Testor's, Pactra, or Humbrol. Humbrol has the widest range of real aircraft colors while the Scalecoat II line is almost exclusively railroad colors.

Experienced modelers almost always mix their paints to match color chips, regardless of the brand of paint they prefer. However, some hobbyists feel that the practice of matching paint colors to actual color samples of the real aircraft is worthwhile only if you are modeling a brand-new aircraft as it left the production line or, perhaps, a modern commercial or private plane that is frequently repainted. Colors change so radically with the weather that it is absurd to assume, for instance, that a World War II-era P-40 really was true Military Specification (MS) colors for more than a week after it left the factory. If you mix your paint to match color paintings (there are thousands of them in books and magazines) or if you can buy a nearly-matching color, then settle for that. There's more information about the research needed to find special paint schemes in Chapter 6.

Here are some hints for mixing paints to achieve the exact color you need. Use an eye dropper to count the drops of paint and record the exact proportions of each color used. It is sometimes easier to start with the primary color closest to the shade you want than to try to make a green, for example, "just a little more blue." When mixing or blending colors, always start with the lightest color and add the darker color, drop by drop, until you have the correct shade. If the color is too dark, add some drops of white; if the color is too light, add drops of black. Remember that the colors will change as they dry. Use these formulas to achieve the correct color:

> Blue plus yellow = green
> Yellow plus red = orange
> Blue plus red = purple
> Blue plus yellow plus red = brown
> Yellow plus red plus black = brown

Primers

A primer is a coat of paint that is intended to be applied directly to the bare surface of the model. It is best to avoid them except in rare cases when you must paint the model white or light yellow and the plastic itself is a very dark color. In this instance, the flat-finish paints can serve the function of conventional primers. A single application of any of the Polly S, Pactra, Testor's, Humbrol or Scalecoat II light grey flat-finish paints will *reduce* the number of color coats that will then be required to completely cover the darker plastic. You may still need two or three coats of white or light yellow but you could use as many as six coats if you skipped the primer step. Floquil paints will work only if you use an airbrush.

The model must be almost surgically clean if you are going to go for the thinnest possible layer of paints. The plastic parts will be coated with a grease that was used at the model kit factory to make it easier for the parts to be released from the mold. In addition, you will have left behind grease from your fingertips when you assembled the model. You can remove the grease and create a built-in type of primer surface in a single process. Mount the model securely on a bent wire coathanger so the hanger can serve as a handle. Hold the model under cool running water in a sink (hot water can warp it!) while you scrub the surface with a toothbrush and kitchen cleanser. Don't scrub too hard because the cleanser can actually scour away some of the finer details. The cleanser will give the smooth plastic a microscopic grain that will help to hold even the water-soluble flat-finish paints securely on the model's surface. Be sure to rinse the model thoroughly to remove all trace of the cleanser. Shake the model and turn it around to remove the bulk of the water. Hang it in a dust-free area for a couple of days until it is completely dry.

Figure 3-1. Bend a wire coat hanger so it will stay inside the model. Bend the other end into a loop for hanging the model after it has been painted.

Painting with a Brush

Every modeler uses a paintbrush to apply paint to the detail areas like landing gear, cockpit interior, and engines, even if the rest of the model was painted with an aerosol can or an airbrush. Buy the best quality sable hair brushes you can find: a number 000 or 00 for the fine details, a number 1 or 2 for general details, and a 1/4-inch wide flat brush for larger areas. Wash the brushes in lacquer thinner after use to remove even the water-soluble paints, then wash them again with soap and warm water. Squeeze all water from the brush and shape its hairs back to the original position. Store the brush either flat or with the hairs upright.

When you dip the brush into the paint, never put more than 1/4 of the length of the brush into the paint bottle, even if you're painting a very large area. You should never, ever, find paint near the metal ferrule of the paintbrush. An accumulation of paint near the base of the brush hairs will soon ruin the brush because you'll leave some paint behind no matter how well you clean the brush. If there's paint at the base of the hairs, you have either dipped the brush too far into the paint bottle or you are using

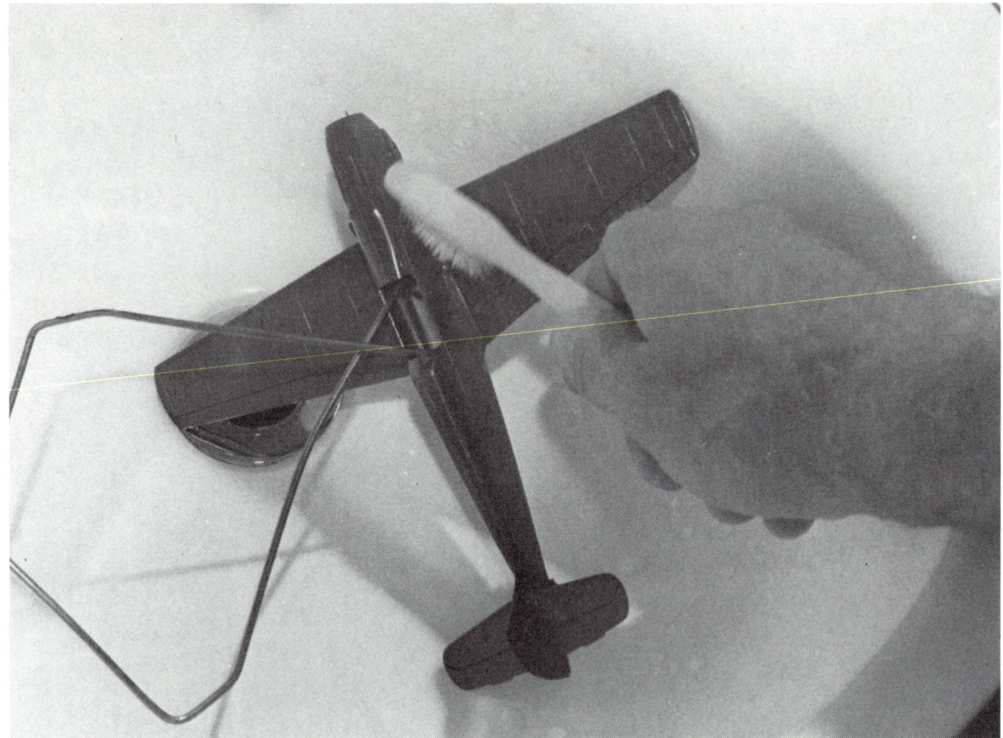

Figure 3-2. Scrub the model with a toothbrush and household kitchen cleanser to clean it and to roughen the surface slightly.

too much pressure when brushing the paint onto the model. If you are painting a very small area, you can gently wipe the brush hairs against the inside of the bottle to squeeze most of the paint from the brush.

All of the bottled paints for models are mixed with enough thinner to be just right for most brush work. If the paint appears to leave brush marks because it's too thick, give it a chance to dry to determine whether or not the brush marks will even out as the paint dries. If you must add thinner, always use the same brand as the paint. If the paint appears to be too thin, simply apply another coat to obtain the coverage you need.

There are two distinct methods of applying paint with a brush. One school of painting demands that the brush never leave the model when changing directions. The other school requires a slight dabbing technique. In both cases, though, the individual strokes must be as smooth as possible with the brush leaving and touching the model at a very gentle angle to minimize beginning and ending brush marks. It is generally easier to blend the beginnings and endings of the brush strokes with fresh paint after they have dried. If, then, you are painting a very large area, limit the length of your strokes to about two inches and overlap the *sides* of each stroke as well as the ends. If you missed an area or if the paint appears to be too thin, wait until it dries and apply another complete coat of paint. When model paints are applied wet, it's almost impossible to leave brush marks. If you try to go back over paint that is only partially dry, however, you most certainly will leave brush marks.

Mentally divide the aircraft into logical areas so you can complete, for example, the painting of the top of the right wing before moving on to the top of the left wing, and so forth. Do not be concerned if you have managed to leave a few brush marks where fresh brush strokes overlapped partially-dried paint; the two coats of clear paint needed to apply the decals will smooth the surface of the model so all but hair-size brush strokes will disappear.

Special Hand-Painting Techniques   You can achieve some rather interesting paint-blending and camouflage techniques using old paintbrushes with their bristles cut to within 1/8 inch of the metal ferrule. The short-hair paintbrush can be used, with just a touch of paint, to provide a stipple effect. Dab the very ends of the hairs onto the surface so you apply tiny dots of paint. If the paint is thinned with about 9 parts of thinner, you can use this technique to simulate the blending of two colors that appears at the color separation lines on most camouflage schemes. Thicker paint, right from the bottle, can be used to create some of the mottled camouflage patterns used by the German and Italian fighters during World War II.

This same mottling technique can be performed with small pieces of sponge. Sponges are available in a wide variety of pore sizes. You might

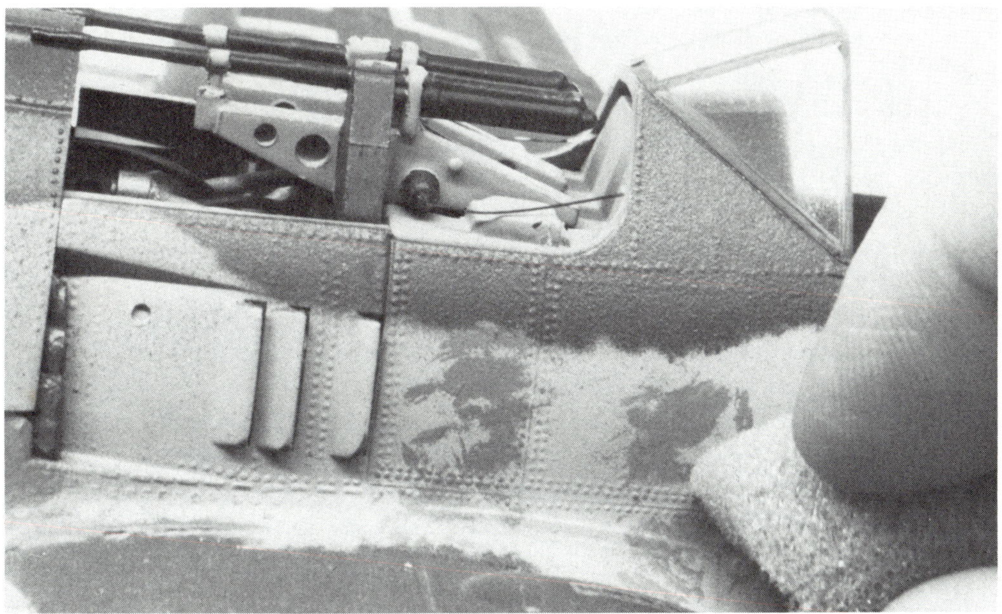

Figure 3-3. This type of camouflage is easy to apply if you use a sponge dipped into paint and dab on the color.

want to try everything from pinhole-size pores to the pea-size pores in natural sponges. Dab just a touch of full-strength or thinned paint when using the sponge.

Painting with Aerosol Cans

Spray painting can take the tedium out of finishing any aircraft model. Most modelers also find it much easier to obtain a smooth and even coat on their miniatures when the paint is applied as a spray. Most of the colors that are available in bottles are also available in aerosol cans from Pactra and Testor's. Again, use *only* flat-finish colors for your miniatures. The only way to mix special colors for spray painting is with the use of an airbrush. This is one of the primary reasons for the popularity of airbrushes among miniature aircraft modelers. Spray painting is not a magical answer to a fine finish. You'll still have to use some of the tricks that modelers have developed and acquire lots of practice to get a perfect finish every time.

The Setup   There are some hazards and special problems inherent in any type of spray painting. Spray painting tends to atomize and spread the solvents in the paint so you must have some effective means of circulating the air. All spray painting must be done either outdoors or in an area well away from any flames with a vent fan to pull the fumes out through an open window or vent. You may also need to wear a respirator mask so the paint and fumes are not inhaled. Paint supply stores sell masks with disposable filters that house painters use. The force of the spray paint will also circulate any dust around the paint area so you must work in a perfectly clean area. It's wise to wipe the surfaces of your spray booth or vent hood with a wet rag, leaving a slight bit of moisture behind, just before you paint.

You'll need some means of holding the model and the parts while they are being painted. A bent coathanger works fine to hold a completed aircraft model. A scrap of 1/4 x 2 wood lath with masking tape can be used as a holder for small parts. Just tuck the ends of the tape under, as shown in figure 3-4, to hold the masking tape to the board with its sticky side facing upward. All the small parts can then be attached to the tape by simply pressing them in place. Some of the parts may have to be painted twice to get paint coverage on the side that was on the tape. Make sure the painted side is dry before placing it on the tape.

Build a spray booth by taping open the top of a corrugated cardboard carton, or make a spray booth out of an inexpensive household stove hood. Upend the hood, placing it on the side that would normally be attached to the wall. Into its heater stack add a section of the flexible hose used with clothes dryers, and add an outside vent to that (see figure 3-6). Inside the hood, where you will be spraying, insert a furnace filter to catch paint spray particles. You should build a spray booth even if you are

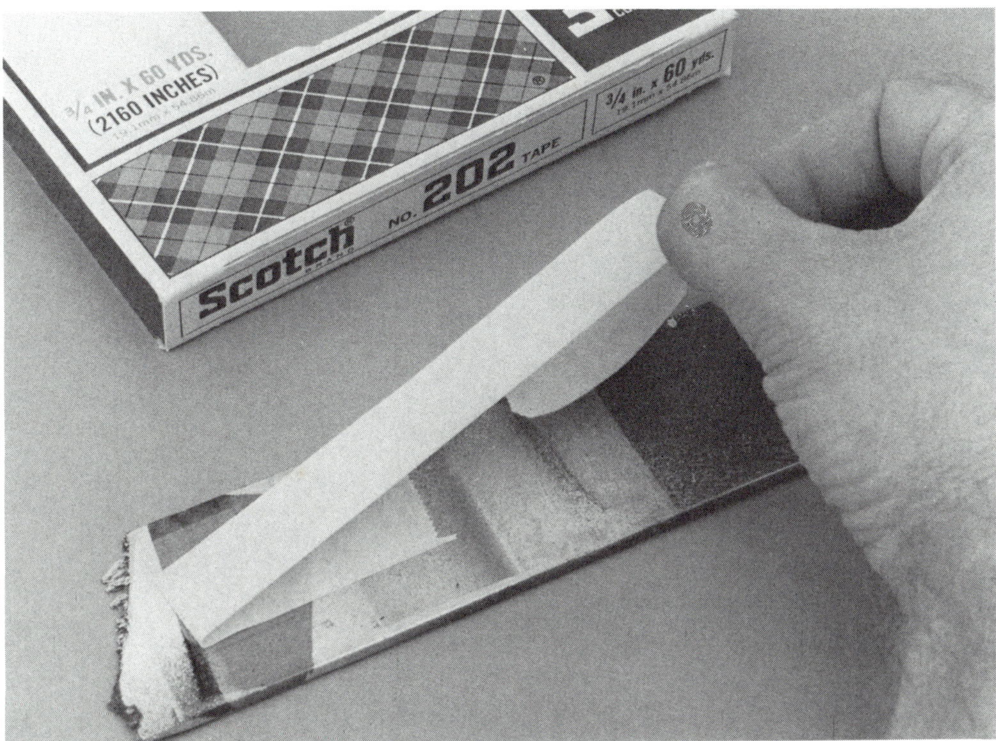

Figure 3-4. Apply a strip of masking tape with the tape's sticky side up to use a scrap of wood as a painting rack.

brush-painting your models; the clear paints needed for the decals *must* be sprayed on the miniature.

You'll also need to have a second large box with hooks to hold the model on its coathanger or the boards with painted pieces taped on while the paint dries. This booth will keep the dust off the model until it dries. Bend a hook in the hanger holding the airplane and drill a hole in the tape-covered painting board so these can be suspended from the hooks in the drying booth. If you're using a modified kitchen vent hood, you can simply leave the fan on for a few hours while the model and parts hang from hooks taped to the upper edge of the hood.

Technique   The secret of applying paint from an aerosol can is to judge just how far the paint nozzle must be from the model and how fast you must move the spray of paint over the model. The spray must be allowed to pass over the model just slowly enough so the paint accumulates to the point where it barely begins to appear wet. You cannot hold the spray in one place because the paint will become so thick it will run before you have a chance to turn the can away. Try holding the can roughly a foot from the model and passing the spray over the model at about the

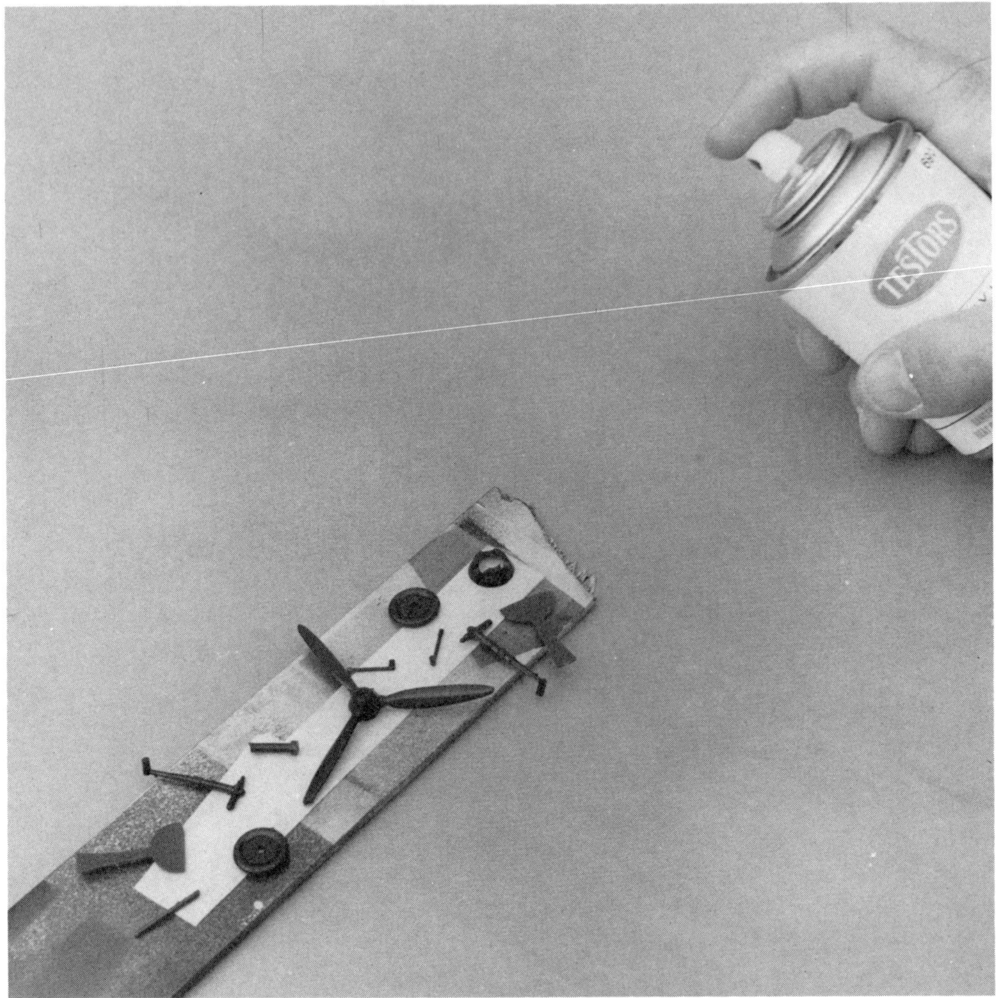

Figure 3-5. The smaller parts can be held to the sticky side of the masking tape while you spray paint them.

same speed as you are reading this line of words. If the resulting paint is dry, try moving the can a bit slower and/or try holding it an inch or more closer. If the paint is so wet it begins to run, try moving the can a bit quicker and/or try holding it a little further away. You'll have to perform this type of experiment with *every* aerosol can because each one, even the same color from the same paint manufacturer, will have a slightly different force.

The paint will sputter and splatter a bit when you first press the nozzle and when you let up on the nozzle. You should always start the spray off to one side of the model, pass it smoothly and evenly over the model, and continue spraying until the paint is off the model. One of the reasons

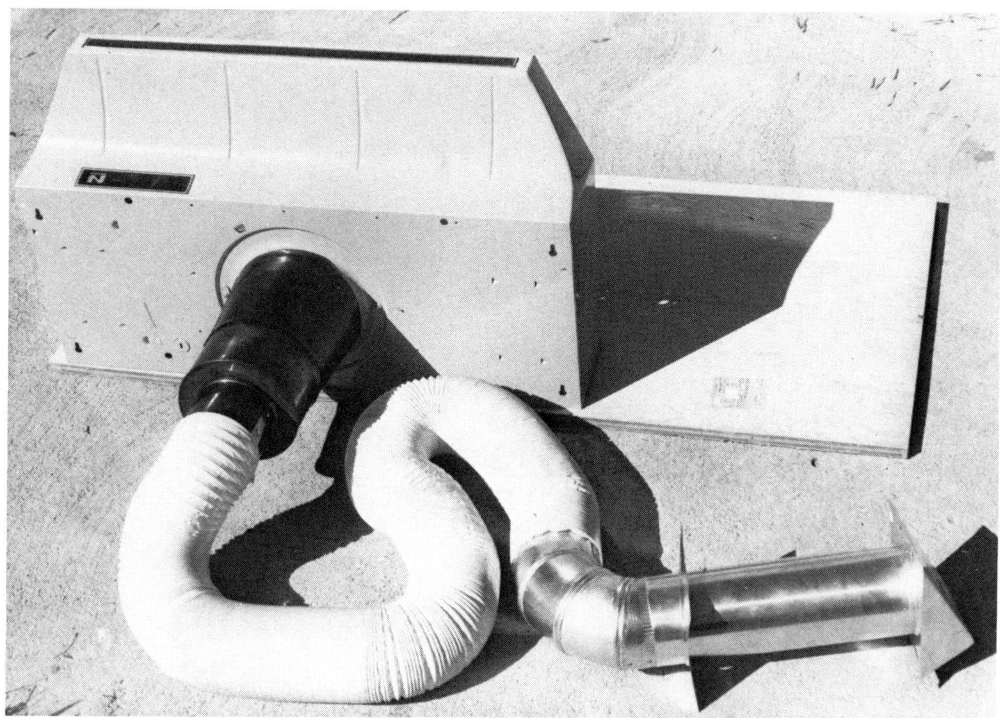

Figure 3-6. This paint spray booth was constructed from a stove hood, and its vent stack was adapted for ventilation from a clothes dryer vent.

CAUTION: Any electric motor used in a vent or paint spray booth must be the explosion-proof type. The motors in most kitchen vent hoods are seldom this type and must be replaced with an explosion-proof motor before allowing paint fumes near the vent hood or motor.

Figure 3-7. The spraying side of the stove hood has a stick-on fluorescent light fixture in place of the usual incandescent light. The furnace filters catch excess paint particles.

Figure 3-8. Hold the aerosol spray can of paint 9 to 12 inches from the model, moving the model rather than the paint can.

for using a spray booth is to catch all that oversprayed paint. You will have to maneuver the model around under the spray because the spray can *must* remain nearly upright all the time you are using it. It can be a lot easier to just hold the spray can in one place and move the model back and forth and around under the spray. When you have finished spraying, turn the can upside down and depress the nozzle until the color stops coming from the nozzle. The compressed air inside the can will clean the nozzle automatically with this technique.

Masking Techniques

Almost every aircraft is painted in at least two colors, so the modeler, like the builder of the full-size aircraft, must find some way of covering or masking the first color while the second color is being applied. If you are painting the entire model with paintbrushes, you need only be concerned with the masking techniques described later for making the braces on canopies. The line that marks the point where one color stops and the other begins is called the color separation line. On commercial and private aircraft, that line is usually sharp and even; on most warplanes, the color separation lines are almost always a hazy blending of the two colors. The techniques for making a crisp color separation line are the same whether you are spraying the paint from an aerosol can or an airbrush. It takes some tricks, though, to simulate the hazy or blended color separation lines if you are using aerosol cans.

Color Separation Lines   There are two proven methods of masking a model to produce a crisp color separation line: using clear Scotch Magic tape to mask-off the first color or using a masking fluid like Micro Scale's Micro Mask or Cary's Magic Masker. The fluids are a type of water-soluble rubber cement that can be brushed on and, when dry, peeled off without damage to the model. On some models you may even want to combine both methods, using the Magic tape for a cover on large areas and masking fluid for the complex edges of camouflage patterns or canopies. The fluids are also helpful when you must mask a compound curve like the nose of a commercial jet or a bullet-shaped propellor spinner. Do *not* try to cut the tape or brush the masking fluid into the shape of the wavy lines of a camouflage pattern. Cover the entire surface with the Magic tape or the masking fluid, then (after the fluid is dry) cut the color separation line through the mask and peel back the excess tape or dried masking fluid.

When you are spraying two colors, always start with the lighter of the two even if only a small portion of that color will be visible. Allow the first color at least two days to dry before applying the masking fluid or tape and the second color. The tape can be removed as soon as the model is dry enough to be handled without leaving fingerprints in the paint. Before removing the tape, however, slice through the paint along the color separation line using the tape or the dried masking fluid to guide your blade—only very gentle pressure will be needed to cut through the layer of paint. This technique insures that you will peel back only the tape, not part of the color. When you peel the tape away, pull it directly back over itself, not straight upward, to minimize the chances of removing some of

Figure 3-9. When you remove Scotch Magic tape from a masked area, pull the tape directly back over itself as shown.

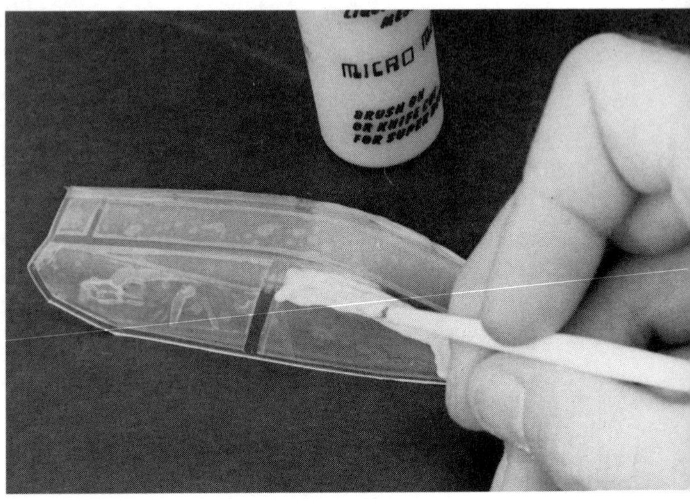

Figure 3-10. The clear areas of this helicopter canopy will be painted with Micro Mask liquid masking fluid. Cover the inside of the canopy with Scotch Magic tape before spray painting.

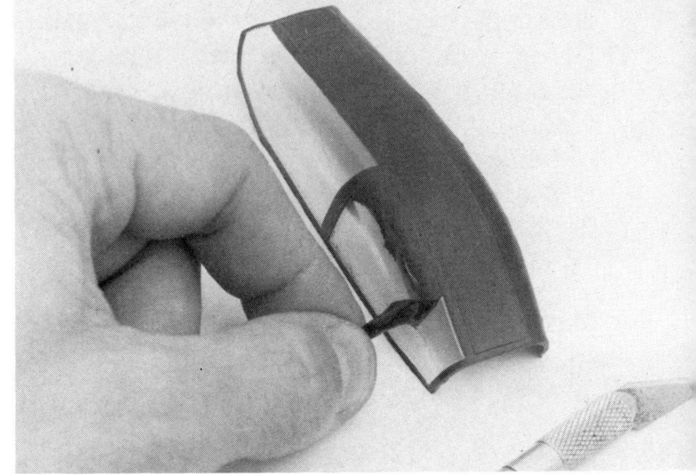

Figure 3-11. Spray paint the canopy and, when the paint is barely dry, slice along the edges of the window, then peel off the masking fluid.

the first color with the tape. If you do remove some of the first color, then you probably did not allow enough time for it to dry completely before covering it with tape, or you failed to clean the model properly before applying that first color.

Clear Canopies and Windows This type of masking technique is extremely effective in duplicating the painted frames around clear canopies or windows. Cover the entire clear canopy or window area and frame with either Scotch Magic tape or masking fluid. Slice through the tape or dried fluid all along the edges of the canopy frame. Carefully peel back the tape or fluid so the entire canopy frame is exposed, leaving the tape or fluid only over the portions that you wish to remain clear. Be sure to mask-off the entire underside of the canopy or window. Spray paint the entire canopy or window area. When the paint is dry, trace the edges of the frames once again with a hobby knife to slice through the paint. Finally,

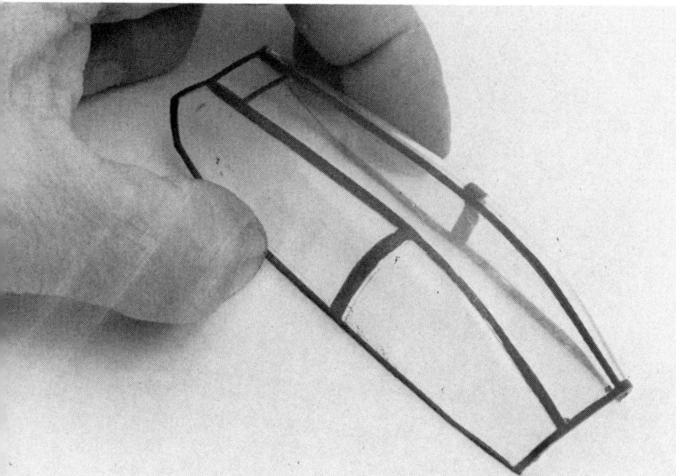

Figure 3-12. When all of the masking fluid is peeled away, the paint will remain only on the canopy braces.

Figure 3-13. The canopy can now be cemented to the model.

peel away the tape or dried masking fluid from the areas you want to remain clear. The canopy can now be installed on the model. (This same method can be used to paint the canopy *after* it is installed.) This technique is especially useful when windows, like those in a commercial jet, must be masked and painted.

The only sensible alternative to this method is to form the framework of the canopy with Scotch Magic tape. Lay several inches of the tape on a piece of glass and spray the tape the proper color. Next, slice through the tape and paint to cut the tape into strips the width of the canopy framework. The tape can then be pressed into place over the clear plastic canopy frames and trimmed to shape.

Blended Camouflage Patterns   The secret to producing a blended color separation line for camouflage patterns is to hold the mask about 1/16 inch away from the surface of the model. This will allow only a

Figure 3-14. Thin strips of Scotch Magic tape, painted to match the aircraft and cut with a knife, have been used on this canopy.

Figure 3-15. Use a rag, held against the edges of the wings and fuselage, to mask the model for a hazy color separation line.

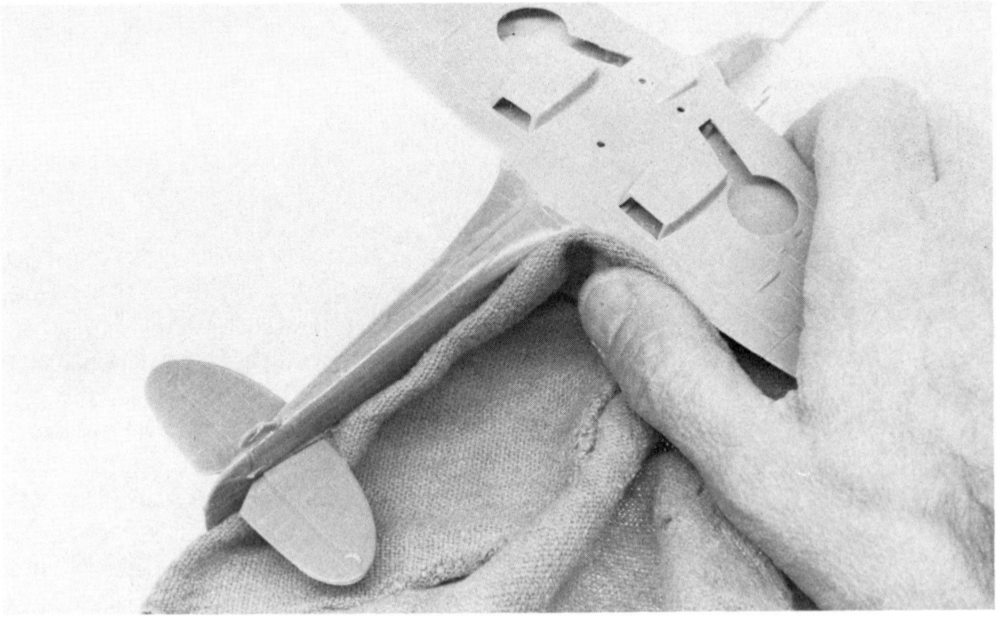

Figure 3-16. Cut wavy camouflage patterns from a sheet of paper. Copy scale-size versions of actual aircraft camouflage.

Figure 3-17. Hold the paper about 1/16 inch from the surface of the aircraft with masking tape folded over itself or rolled into a thin tube. Spray paint at a 90° angle to the paper to obtain a hazy-edged color separation line.

portion of the paint to reach the aircraft, producing the hazy or blended type of color separation. If you are merely masking-off the upper portion of the fuselage and the tops of the wings, you can simply hold a rag in place while you spray the lighter color. Do hold the rag or mask with a glove so you don't spray your hand as well as the model.

The more intricate camouflage patterns can be cut into a piece of paper. Fold a piece of masking tape over itself and use it to hold the paper 1/16 inch away from the model while you spray on the darker color. When the paint dries, remove the paper mask and reuse it for the second wing and for the stabilizer.

Chapter 4

Airbrushing Techniques

THE airbrush is a tool that functions like a miniature version of the spray guns used to paint full-size automobiles and houses. Artists use airbrushes to create soft-edge and shadow effects for illustrations but the tool is equally useful for painting true-to-scale paint schemes on miniature aircraft. The airbrush is a considerable improvement over the aerosol spray can in finishing models. The airbrush allows you to vary the amount of thinner, it allows you to mix special colors, and you can adjust the air and paint supply so you can apply a paint pattern as small as the period in this sentence. It combines the best features of the paintbrush and the aerosol can to make painting a pleasure. Only with a tremendous amount of skill and practice can you come close to duplicating the blended edge effects of an airbrush with a spray can or a paintbrush. The airbrush is a tool for those who are really serious about their modeling efforts because the only acceptable airbrush outfits sell for between $100 and $200, figures that definitely place them in the "optional" class.

The Airbrush Outfit

You can purchase a tool called an airbrush for as little as $11. These inexpensive airbrushes mix the air with the paint externally: one nozzle directs the paint toward the air nozzle on the tip of the airbrush so the air pulls the paint up and mixes it with air to atomize the paint. There is very little adjustment possible with the paint spray from this type of airbrush and the paint is not atomized as completely as it is with more expensive airbrushes. The only advantage a cheap airbrush offers over an aerosol can is that you can mix colors or thinner into the paint. Since most of the expense of an airbrush outfit is the air supply, I'd suggest you avoid the external mix airbrushes for model building.

The single-action airbrush most modelers prefer sells for about $35, and is sufficient for painting models if you don't want a double-action brush. The single-action airbrushes sold by firms like Badger, Paasche, Binks, and Thayer and Chandler also have internal mixing of the air and paint. The push button controls only the flow of air; a knob or screw must be turned to adjust the flow of paint through the brush.

Artists prefer a double-action airbrush that mixes the paint and air

Figure 4-1. Dan Wilson used an airbrush and a paintbrush to paint this Revell 1/72-scale Me109E-4 to match one that flew from Derna, Libya in 1941.

inside the brush for complete atomization of the paint. This type of airbrush has a push button that can be depressed to control the air flow and pulled like a trigger to control the paint flow. This means you can start painting a dot the size of a period, lead away from that dot with a pencil-thin line and expand the line into a baseball-size pattern without touching anything but that push button. The double-action airbrushes sell for between $30 and $100; $60 is about average.

I find that it is quite easy to accidentally pull the push button on the double-action airbrushes and then end up with too much or too little paint. However, when you have become proficient in the use of the airbrush, you may want to have the advantage of push-button paint flow control. The pull-back action of the button on most double-action airbrushes can be locked in place with a rubber band or a small piece of masking tape while you learn to use the airbrush as though it were a single-action type. When you've mastered this, you can remove the rubber band or tape and use the pull-back action of the push button to vary the flow of paint while you vary the flow of air by pushing down on the button.

The air supply for your airbrush is as important a purchase as the airbrush itself. You must have an air supply with an adjustable air pressure (pounds per square inch or "psi") and with a steady supply of air with no fluctuations or pulsing. Air compressors with electric motors of 1/12 horsepower sell for as little as $50, and larger models that have their own air tanks sell for as much as $150. You will also need a pressure relief or "bleeder" valve (for compressors that do not have an air tank) to help dampen the surges or pulses of air from the compressor pump; this will cost about $6 to $10. The bleeder valve dispenses excess air pressure from the compressor into the air to help keep the flow of air as smooth as possible. You will also need an adjustable air pressure valve with a gauge ($25 to $50) and you will probably need a moisture trap if you live in a humid climate ($20 to $40).

I use an old oxygen tank that a welding supply firm modified with a tank capacity (pressure) gauge and an air supply valve with pressure gauge that I use as a "silent compressor". The tank needs to be refilled only about once every three years but the initial cost was more than that of an air compressor outfit. I cannot recommend the use of the aerosol cans of propellant because there is no accurate way of controlling their air pressure.

Painting with an Airbrush

You will need to use the same type of ventilated spray booth with an airbrush that you use with aerosol cans. You should also use the same means of holding the models and the parts. The mess from oversprayed paint should be much less with an airbrush than with aerosol cans because more of the paint will land on the model, thanks to the well-controlled spray pattern of an airbrush.

If you can apply paint successfully with aerosol cans, you'll find working with an airbrush to be a sheer delight because you really can control the paint pattern and can apply the paint almost as accurately as you can with a paintbrush. The size of the paint pattern is determined by the distance between the airbrush and the model. You can adjust the paint and air supply with an airbrush so you can hold the brush as close as two inches from the model (for spraying small areas or camouflage patterns) or as far as 18 inches away (to spray large areas). The airbrush is not an automatic tool, though; you must make adjustments in both the air and paint supply to use the tool effectively. If you have a choice of nozzle sizes when you purchase your airbrush, pick the medium size (usually a B or 2).

I would suggest you start with an air pressure of about 25 psi (pounds per square inch), and with 3 parts of bottled paint mixed with one part of the same brand of thinner. This combination will give you something close to the effect of using an aerosol can so you'll be starting on familiar ground. The paint-flow adjusting screw on the airbrush will have to be turned in or out to produce a spray of paint about four inches in diameter when the work is about a foot away from the airbrush nozzle. Paint something (like an empty kit box) with the airbrush on these settings to get the feel of the paint spray and the push button's effect. Do not try to regulate the flow of air by pushing the button only part of the way down; if you need less air, turn the knob on the air pressure gauge to reduce or increase the air pressure. Adjust the air pressure and the paint-flow screw until the airbrush feels like the old familiar aerosol can of paint.

When you're able to work with five variables—spray distance, duration of spray, air pressure, paint flow, and the amount of thinner—you may still find yourself confused. Make a note of the air pressure and paint flow settings that feel right to you so you can return to them as a "control" or "standard" if you do get confused. These standard settings can also be used to help identify any problems with an erratic airbrush paint pattern. You should be able to pinpoint whether the problem is being created by internal clogging in the airbrush or by some fault in the air supply. You will achieve the best results with your airbrush if you go on and learn the

Figure 4-2. Adjust the airbrush paint-flow and the air supply pressure to match the feel of an aerosol can while you are learning to use the air brush.

airbrush techniques that make the tool so useful to aircraft modelers. Even if you just learn to use the airbrush like an aerosol can, however, you'll still have the advantages of being able to mix your own colors and to vary the amount of thinner.

Mixing Paint for Airbrush Use

There are two entirely different approaches to the use of an airbrush: the first can be called the cautious school and the second the do-it school. The advocates of the cautious approach assume that meticulous care and preparation will yield meticulous-appearing results. The advocates of the do-it approach assume that some mistakes are inevitable and that, if they occur, they can easily be corrected during the remainder of the finishing process. It's a matter of patience: you either have the patience to go through the drill of preparation every time you paint, or you take your chances and have the patience to correct paint spatters or runs after they occur. I've seen International Plastic Modelers Society (IPMS) contests where winners in different eras of miniature aircraft came from *both* of these schools of thought. Try both approaches to see which yields the best results for you.

The cautious modeler begins by mixing the paint. The first color is mixed thoroughly both by stirring, then by shaking the bottle. This color

Figure 4-3. Use an eye dropper to count the number of drops of each color that you are mixing.

is then transferred into an empty bottle using a medicine dropper to measure the exact amount of paint desired. I generally fill the bottle as close to half-full as possible with the available paint. To be safe, hold a tea strainer over the mouth of the bottle to strain out any coagulated lumps of paint or other debris. Bottles with screw-on caps that fit most brands of airbrushes are available from the airbrush companies or through your hobby dealer. Next, add enough thinner to give that 3:1 paint-to-thinner proportion (or whatever mixture you prefer) and shake the bottle vigorously once again. If you purchased extra bottles, this one can be labeled with the color, the proportion of thinner, and the date so you can duplicate the color later if you need more paint. Adjust the air pressure to your favorite setting (try 25 psi for starters) and test the action of the airbrush on a piece of white paper while you adjust the paint flow valve.

The do-it school of airbrushing relies on the element of chance, hoping that there will be very few times when the paint will clog the airbrush because it is too thick or because it was not run through the tea strainer to remove any lumps. You can spray most of the Floquil (but not Polly S), Pactra, and Testor's flat colors without adding any thinner if you open the paint flow needle on the airbrush far enough and if you are using a medium (size B or 2) or a large nozzle. The paint usually will begin to clog the airbrush sometime during the spraying process, but you can almost always stop that by simply opening the paint flow valve on the airbrush a bit more. If you catch the clogging soon enough, there is very little chance that the airbrush will become so clogged that you must stop and clean it. If you cannot prevent the clogging by adjusting the air brush, then you'll just have to add thinner. This method can only be used to produce flat finishes, however; it will not work well with glossy paints or with the semi-gloss Scalecoat paints. I have found it necessary to add at least one part thinner to two parts paint (equal parts of paint and thinner are better) when trying to achieve a perfectly smooth semi-gloss or a simulated aluminum finish. I have also found it necessary to thin even the flat-finish Humbrol and Polly S paints for use in the airbrush. I use unthinned paints so often that I've modified several bottle caps so I can simply screw a well-mixed bottle of most brands of flat-finish paint onto my airbrush and spray away.

Super-Smooth Finishes

The best possible method for achieving a super-smooth finish on a model is to use gloss rather than flat paints. Your airbrush will give you an advantage here because you can apply a much thinner and more even coat of gloss paint with your airbrush than you could using that same brand of paint from an aerosol can. Testor's or Pactra gloss-finish paints should be thinned with one part lacquer thinner and one part mineral spirits to two parts paint.

Lloyd Jones, one of the top ten aircraft model builders in the world, has developed a technique using this paint mixture at an unusually low 8 psi of air pressure. The paint flow will have to be adjusted, of course, for an even spray at that pressure. Many of Lloyd's models are replicas of commercial airliners with large areas of white. If the model to be painted has any areas of white or light pastel colors, Lloyd applies a primer coat of aluminum (usually the non-buffing variety of Spray-N-Plate) followed by the white or pastel color. Darker colors are applied last. The gloss finish is nearly as thin as the flat-finish paints and he avoids the need to apply a coat of clear before the decals are positioned. Lloyd doesn't even apply clear on top of the decals. Every brand of clear flat or clear gloss paint he knows of will eventually yellow a bit. If you must use a clear, I've found that the Flecto Varathane paint yellows less than any other but you must use the brush-on variety; the aerosol cans do seem to yellow and the fluid attacks most decals. The Varathane can be applied with an airbrush, of course, thinned with lacquer thinner and mineral spirits like the color coats of paint.

Cleaning Your Airbrush

It is possible to ruin an airbrush if you allow it to become clogged too often, or if you fail to clean it after *every* color change and when you are through painting. It's not the paint that ruins the airbrush, but the wear on the parts from constant scrubbing of hardened paint. If you are careful enough (and quick enough to open the paint flow valve) to avoid any clogging and if you do clean the airbrush every time you spray a different color, then you should not have to disassemble the airbrush more than once or twice a year. Some manufacturers do recommend that their airbrushes be disassembled for every cleaning and you may void any warranty if you do not follow their instructions.

Most modelers remove the plastic syphon tube to clean inside it with a pipe cleaner and thinner, and they remove the needle-protector so they can clean dried paint from around the needle. The paint tends to dry in those two areas, it seems, even more than inside the airbrush itself. When you do disassemble your airbrush, follow the manufacturer's instructions carefully. Be particularly careful not to allow even the slightest scratch on any of the internal parts or you may ruin the air brush.

The day-to-day cleaning of your airbrush is quite easy. If the airbrush is not clogged and no completely dry paint is inside of it, it can be cleaned simply by spraying thinner through it to flush all of the orifices clear of paint. Attach a jar of thinner in place of the jar of paint. Spray the thinner into an old rag, a tissue or a paper towel until no more color appears. Hold the rag or paper over the nozzle to block all of the air holes; this will force the air backward through the airbrush to create bubbles in the thinner. You must cover all of the air holes or the process won't work.

Alternately block and unblock the air holes, while the air supply is on and the push button is depressed. This will cause a backward and forward surging of the thinner through the air and paint passages that should thoroughly flush any paint from inside the airbrush. Now clean the dried paint from around the nozzle, the pickup tube, and the paint bottle lid with rags soaked in thinner and pipe cleaners.

I hang my airbrush on a small hook beside the paint booth after using it. When I'm through painting for the day I always cover the nozzle with a protective cap and install an empty bottle to catch any debris from the pickup side of the airbrush. I also turn the air supply completely off. I keep a special jar of thinner for use in the first clean-up of the airbrush. This jar has a small amount of color from previous cleanings that settles to the bottom. For the final cleaning, I use fresh thinner in a clean jar. This saves a whole lot of thinner. When the "dirty" thinner gets too dirty, I set it aside for use in "muddy" weathering effects because, on the average, a random mixture of colors will produce a dark brown that is just fine for simulating engine or gun exhaust stains.

Airbrushing Techniques and Rules

The five airbrushing variables to remember are spray distance, duration of spray, air pressure, paint flow, and the amount of thinner. By adjusting these you can produce paint effects that simulate almost every type of aircraft camouflage and many wear and weather effects.

Unfortunately, you will encounter many problems as you practice your airbrushing technique. There is a large difference in the thickness of even the same brand of paint for modelers. It would seem that some paint pigments cannot be ground as fine or do not mix as well as others. Even the degree of humidity and the barometric pressure on a particular day can affect the adjustments needed to spray a certain pattern with an airbrush. If the temperature in the spray booth is relatively cool, you may need more air pressure and/or more paint flow than if the temperature is warm. Please keep these variables in mind and be ready to make adjustments every time you spray. It's not really difficult to be ready to turn the air pressure valve or the paint flow screw just a bit to bring things back to what you need. Every airbrush is a precision tool and it takes frequent adjustments to make it perform consistently. If you avoid saying "It doesn't work!" and assume instead that "It needs a bit more (or less) air pressure or more (or less) paint flow," then airbrushing will *always* be a pleasure for you.

You must memorize these two fundamental rules of airbrush painting: ALWAYS HOLD THE AIRBRUSH BOTTLE VERTICALLY (if you don't the paint will spill out the vent hole and over your hand) and APPLY ONLY ENOUGH PAINT TO COLOR THE MODEL.

That second rule is one of the true specialties of the airbrush expert. He (and you, with practice) can apply any type of paint so dry that the

Lee Scow turned his 1/72-scale Revell "Hurricane" Mark I into the fabric-covered version of the real aircraft. The visible ribs were added to the model's surface with strips of heat-stretched plastic sprue and filler putty.

Lloyd Jones assembled this vacuum-formed 1/144-scale Griffin kit of the Boeing 377 Stratocruiser, painted it with Spray-N-Plate and polished it. The kit includes Scale-Master Pan American decals and stripes.

The P-47D "Tarheel Hal" is one of the most famous aircraft of World War II. Kevin Suddarth detailed a Monogram 1/48-scale kit and applied Micro Scale's decals.

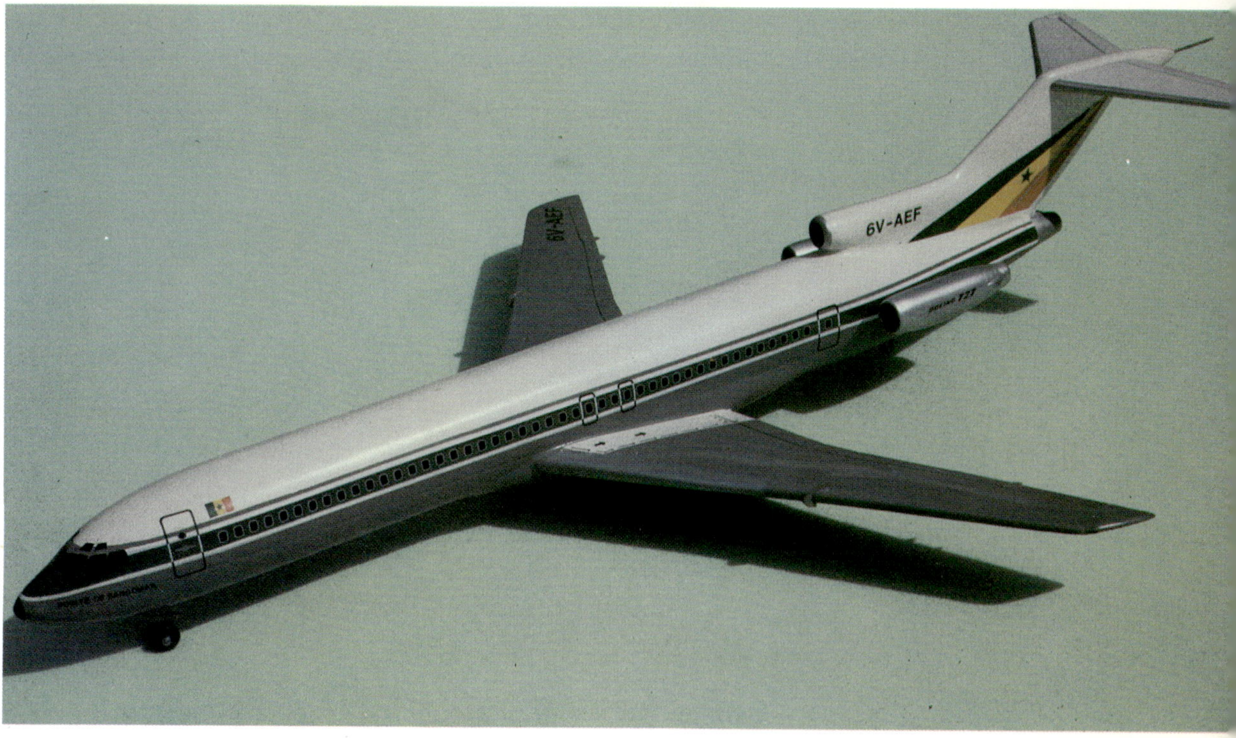

This Boeing 727-200 is an Airfix 1/144-scale 727 that was fitted with a Griffin vacuum-formed conversion kit. Lloyd Jones painted the model and used Scale-Master government of Senegal decals.

Rick Sherry converted his 1/32-scale Hasegawa Fw190A to one of the aircraft that carried the experimental Blohm and Voss Bv246 "Hagelkorn" gliderbomb. He carved the gliderbomb from scrap plastic.

The streaks on the bottom of Rick Sherry's 1/32-scale Revell "Hayate" simulate leaking fuel and hydraulic fluid (red) and flak bursts (black). It represents the real aircraft as it might have appeared near the end of World War II.

The only effective way to duplicate peeling and chipped paint is to apply wax spots on an undercoat of aluminum paint, then paint and peel the final color coat.

Three Messerschmitt Me109s attack a pair of Thunderbolts. The models include a 1/48-scale Fujimi Me109G and a 1/48-scale Monogram P-47D detailed by Kevin Suddarth, a 1/72-scale Hasegawa P-47D built by Dennis Nowicki, a Revell 1/72-scale Me109R-4 by Dan Wilson and a 1/100-scale Me109 built from a Roskopf kit.

This British "Spitfire" Mk V in German markings is an accurate 1/72-scale replica of an aircraft captured during WW II. The model, like the real aircraft, has engine cowls from a Bf110 with an Me109 propeller. Lee Scow did the conversion using three Airfix kits.

Some of the Monogram 1/24-scale Bell "Huey" UH-1B helicopter kits were offered with clear plastic side panels to show the kit's full interior detailing.

This Otaki-brand 1/48-scale P-51D has been painted with Spray-N-Plate aluminum paint with metal pigment, polished to shine like real aluminum, painted and marked with Micro Scale decals by modeler Kevin Suddarth.

Lee Scow cut the stabilizer and rudder control surfaces so they appear to operate, added stretched-sprue rigging and found an authentic black paint scheme for this Lindberg (formerly Pyro) 1/48-scale Gloster "Gladiator."

This Monogram 1/48-scale Mitsubishi A6M5 ''Zero'' was converted to the twin-seat A6M2-K version by cutting the canopies from two kits. Lee Scow also added the wires used on the target-towing ''tug'' version of the real aircraft.

This 1/48-scale Monogram 1937-era Bell P-39 ''Airacobra'' is marked with the tiger-tooth decals included in some of the earlier kits. Lee Scow assembled and detailed the model.

model's surface almost appears to be covered with paint dust rather than paint. With practice, only slightly damp paint pigment will reach the model; the solvents and carriers and thinners will have almost evaporated before the paint reaches the model. This effect is perfect for flat finishes but entirely unsuitable for gloss finishes or for the aluminum paints that can be polished—these paints must be applied just wet enough to flow like brush-on paints.

The airbrush adjustments allow you to control the amount of paint and air to such a degree that you can spray a pattern about the size of a period that, under a powerful magnifying glass, would reveal only about a dozen tiny droplets of paint. The thin lines (f) in figure 4-4, for example, were sprayed with a Badger model 200 (medium nozzle) airbrush with 30 psi of air pressure using black Floquil paint thinned with an equal amount of Floquil Dio Sol. The paint nozzle was only about three inches from the work and the work was moved quite rapidly (about four times as fast as you can read about it) under the paint spray.

Figure 4-4 shows some of the right and wrong ways to spray paint

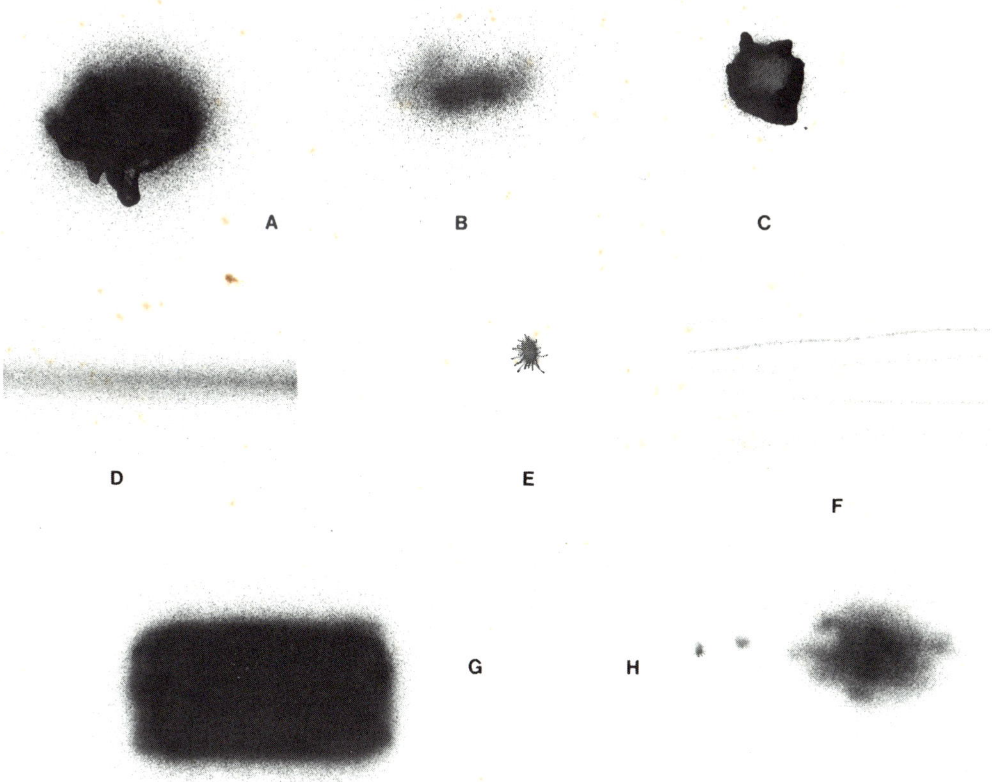

Figure 4-4. These patterns were sprayed with a Badger number 200 single-action airbrush.

with an airbrush. In the top row, from left to right: the first pattern (A) is an example of either holding the pattern in one place too long or holding the nozzle too close to the work; the paint puddled and ran. The middle pattern (B) is an example of too much paint and not enough air pressure, or of holding the nozzle too far from the work. The pattern on the far right (C) is the result of using paint with too much thinner and trying to build up the color by spraying one area for too long; the paint was pushed out from the center by more paint. In the middle row, from left to right: the first pattern (D) is probably a correct adjustment of paint and air but the nozzle was moved over the work too quickly for the paint to color, so it left this pepper pattern. The center pattern (E) was done with the paint flow adjusted to a barely-visible pattern and with 30 psi of air; the goal was to make lines as in the next pattern (F) but the nozzle was held in one place so long the paint accumulated and splattered. The next pattern (F) is an example of five separate passes with the same paint and air setting as the previous pattern but with the work moved very quickly (top), slowly (second line); at medium speeds (third and fourth lines), and at medium speed but twice as far from the nozzle (bottom line). In the bottom row, the first pattern (G) was painted using the same pattern as in the example above it (D), but moving the work much more slowly under the spray, down, then back in six passes; this is one of the proper ways to use an airbrush. The final pattern (H) is an example of the small paint pattern (the two fuzzy dots on its left) to create a hazy or foggy effect by moving the work in a slightly circular motion; this is the pattern to achieve when you are trying to blend, for example, the blue underside of a fighter with an olive drab topside at the two colors' separation line. This same pattern (H) can also be used effectively for many types of camouflage patterns and, with more thinner in the paint, to produce weathering effects.

Generally speaking, you can obtain a smaller paint spray pattern by decreasing the air flow (to as low as 7 psi), decreasing the paint flow, and moving the nozzle as close as an inch from the work. The opacity or degree of coverage of the paint pattern can be made somewhat translucent by moving the work under the spray of paint more rapidly, by adding more thinner to the paint, or by moving the nozzle further away from the work. If you want a very opaque layer of paint (for instance, if you are covering a dark color with a lighter color), try any or all of the following: increase the air flow (to as much as 40 psi); increase the flow of paint; hold the nozzle no more than 12 inches from the work; move the work slowly under the paint spray; use less thinner in the paint. If you remember these guidelines, you'll be able to correct your mistakes and you'll learn to use an airbrush in a short time.

Airbrushing Tips

Because you have five variables to control when airbrushing, there is often more than one place to look when you run into trouble. This list

Figure 4-5. The hazy patterns on this 1/100-scale aircraft were applied with just 15 psi of air pressure and very little paint flow at a distance of three inches from the model.

should help you track down the cause of some common problems. The tips under each problem are given in order, with the most likely cure first.

AIRBRUSH TROUBLE-SHOOTING CHART

If no paint is sprayed:
1. Turn the paint supply screw counterclockwise to increase the available flow of paint.
2. Clean the vent hole in the bottle cap to be certain it is not blocked.
3. Clean the tip and nozzle of the airbrush and, if they were clogged, mix more thinner with the paint.
4. Increase the air pressure to a maximum of 40 psi.

If there is no air:
1. Turn the air supply valve on and adjust the air pressure valve to deliver at least 20 psi.
2. Disconnect the air hose from the airbrush and determine if there is air pressure in the line.
3. Disassemble the airbrush and clean all the air and paint orifices.

If the paint runs or splatters:
1. Move the airbrush further away from the work.
2. Move the work more quickly beneath the paint pattern.
3. Turn the paint supply screw clockwise to decrease the available supply of paint.
4. Reduce the air pressure to a minimum of 7 psi.
5. Add more paint to thicken the paint/thinner mixture.

If the paint is rough or peppery:
1. Move the airbrush closer to the work.
2. Move the work more slowly beneath the paint pattern.
3. Turn the paint supply screw counterclockwise to increase the available supply of paint.
4. Increase the air pressure to a maximum of 40 psi.
5. Add more thinner to the paint.

If the spray pattern is uneven:
1. Clean the nozzle by spraying through it and swabbing it with a pipe cleaner.
2. Remove the paint bottle, cap it, and shake it vigorously to mix the paint.
3. Disassemble the airbrush and inspect it to be certain the needle is not bent or nicked and that all the orifices are clean and unscratched.
4. Add a water trap to the air supply to remove excessive moisture.

If the air surges:
1. Use a longer and larger-diameter air hose between the air compressor and the airbrush to help even out the pulses from the compressor.
2. Install an air supply tank or reservoir between the air compressor and the airbrush.

Chapter 5

Decal and Lining Techniques

A DECAL can almost work magic on a miniature aircraft. The special decals sold in the more expensive kits and those available as extras at hobby shops are no thicker than a coat of paint, and they are almost always accurate replicas of one particular full-size aircraft's markings. When the decal application is completed using the methods in this chapter, it is virtually impossible to tell that the decal was not painted on the model's surface. The decal will conform to every rivet or seam or contour of the model just as tightly as the paint itself. With practice, you can make better stripes with decals than you could ever hope to make using paint and masking techniques.

The Decal Library

There are several thousand different plastic model aircraft currently available and there are several times that many decals. Most aircraft modelers invest in all the decal catalogs they can find so they'll know exactly what is available. When they see a photograph of a particular full-size aircraft they would like to model, they can determine if it is possible to duplicate that aircraft's markings with either stock or modified decals. The decals, like the model kits, are most numerous in 1/72 scale but there are varieties for 1/144, 1/100, 1/87 (model railroad), 1/48, and 1/32-scale kits. The decal manufacturers are clever enough to follow up most new kit introductions with a decal sheet that offers several variations on the markings in the kit.

The range of decals, again like the range of kits, encompasses every era and includes decals for war planes, between-the-wars (the 1930s) planes, commercial aircraft, and some private aircraft. In some instances, particularly if you're building a collection of commercial aircraft, it's worthwhile to buy every kit you see of your potential favorites. The model kit makers quite frequently offer their kits with a number of different decals over the years. If you miss one of the models, you may have to pay dearly for it when it reaches "collector's" age (usually about three years after it is off the market). Micro Scale and Scale-Master have the most popular and extensive ranges of decals in America. You may find ABT, Stoppel, Model Decals, ESCI and other imported brands of decals in some of the hobby shops that specialize in imported miniature aircraft and military kits.

Figure 5-1. These Israeli Air Force markings are just one example of the thousands of special decals for miniature aircraft.

Figure 5-2. Save any leftover decals from kits for use on other types of aircraft miniatures.

How to Apply Decals

A decal is really just several layers of clear and colored paint that are attached to a paper backing with water-soluble glue. When you soak the decal in water, that glue softens. When you apply the decal to the model, that same glue is supposed to hold it in place. The decal-softening fluids help the relatively stiff decal conform to the rivets, panel lines and curves of the model. None of the decal softening fluids is powerful enough to completely melt the decal's paint—they merely soften it into goo.

Preparing the Model for Decals   If you try to apply a decal on a model that has been painted with flat-finish paints, the rough surface of the paint will leave microscopic air bubbles beneath a decal, even one that has been treated with softening fluid. Those air bubbles are what give many decals the appearance of being hazy or foggy. The very feature that makes the flat-finish paint flat is what makes the surface create air bubbles beneath the decal. If you look at the flat-finish paints after they have dried, you'll see what looks like a bed of sand over the surface of the model. It is that sandy effect that prevents light from reflecting off the flat-finish paints and gives them their flat appearance. You must spray a coat of clear gloss (or semi-gloss) paint over the model to fill in around those paint particles so the decal can adhere properly.

Please don't think you can skip a step by painting your model with glossy paints in the first place. The gloss in these paints is achieved by mixing in a rather large proportion of clear paint. All of the gloss paints, then, are somewhat transparent so it takes a very thick layer of paint to cover the model. Believe me, you will have a much thinner layer of paint on your model if you brush or spray on one or two color coats followed by a single coat of clear gloss and, after the decals are applied, a final coat of clear gloss, clear semi-gloss or clear flat paint to achieve the finish that matches the aircraft you are modeling. Those three or four coats of paint will total just a fraction of the thickness of a single coat of high-gloss enamel.

Both of the clear coats *must* be applied with either an aerosol can or an airbrush. If you try to brush on the clear coat you will force it to build up around the detail areas and it will probably attack the decals. Test whatever brand of clear paint you choose on a small area of the kit box that you have painted with the same paint as the model and that has a leftover scrap of the decals applied to it. Some brands of clear paint will attack or etch paints, while others will wrinkle and curl decals. *Every* clear I have tried clouds or etches clear plastic windows or canopies so you *must* either install the clear parts after *both* coats of clear paint have been applied, or mask the clear parts until both coats of clear paint are applied.

I have found very few paints or decals that will be attacked by Testor's aerosol clear flat Dullcote or clear gloss Glosscote, or Pactra's clear flat and clear gloss sprays. I find that Testor's Dullcote gives a very flat finish while Pactra's clear flat gives a semi-gloss finish. The Testor's Dullcote and Glosscote in bottles are relatively new products so I cannot comment on their use. Frankly, there is very little advantage in using an airbrush to apply clear finishes when these aerosol products are available. The clear paints must cover the entire model and the spray from the aerosol can is quite adequate. The coats of clear paint applied with aerosol cans seem to be at least as thin as those applied with an airbrush.

I have seen models that were covered with floor or furniture wax in place of the clear gloss paint but I cannot recommend this practice; if the model is ever subjected to a change in humidity, there is a very good chance the wax beneath (or on top of) the decals would become cloudy and the model would have to be stripped and repainted. If you want to apply a coating of wax to protect the model, do so *after* the final coat of clear gloss or clear flat has dried for about a month. You can achieve some very nice semi-gloss effects, particularly on bare aluminum finishes, by applying just a bit of paste wax over *flat* clear paint (again, after the paint has dried for a month).

Applying the Decals   There really is only one correct way to apply decals so they'll appear as though they were painted on the surface of the model. This is not difficult but it will take patience and practice.

First, each individual decal must be cut from the decal sheet. Hold the decal sheet so it reflects light to determine if the clear or glossy portion covers the entire sheet or if it ends about 1/32 inch from the colored portion of each decal. If the gloss covers the sheet, then you must cut each decal as close as you possibly can to the colored portion so there is little, if any, gloss remaining. If the gloss ends 1/32 inch from the colored portion of the decal then *do not* cut into the gloss. In this type of decal the gloss has a tapered or feathered edge to make the decal look smoother after that final coat of clear paint. Trim these decals about 1/16 inch or more away from the colored portion so you won't slice through the gloss. Be sure to have nearby the box art or the book or magazine you will use as a reference for the decal application. Most modelers find they can place decals more accurately using the eyeball method then by measuring from a plan or profile view. Once the decals are cut apart, you will handle them *only* with tweezers, never with your fingers.

Pick up a decal with tweezers and dip it into a cup of warm water for no more than 10 to 15 seconds, then place the decal face up on a blotter or a piece of paper towel. Soak only the decals for the tops of the wings *or* for the right side of the fuselage right now. Leave the decal on the blotter or paper towel for a minute or two until the water soaks through the decal's paper backing to dissolve the glue. In the meantime, brush a layer of decal softener, like Micro Scale's Micro Set, Walthers' Solvaset, Champion's Decal Set, or Testor's Decal Set over the surface of the model where you want to place that first decal. Pick up the decal with tweezers after you have determined that it can be moved on its paper backing (if not, wait another minute and try again). Position both the decal and the paper backing over the wet area where the decal is to rest. Hold the decal in place with the tip of a hobby knife or a second pair of tweezers while you pull the paper backing out from under the decal with tweezers. Brush a second coat of decal softener over the face of the decal (use the same brand of softener under and on top of the decal; for instance, use Micro Sol on top if you put Micro Set beneath the decal). Position the decal precisely where you want it. If there is so much water or decal softening fluid that the decal is literally floating, touch a corner of a facial tissue to the edge of the fluid (don't touch the decal!) and let the tissue absorb the excess fluid.

Repeat this procedure with all of the decals on one of the model's

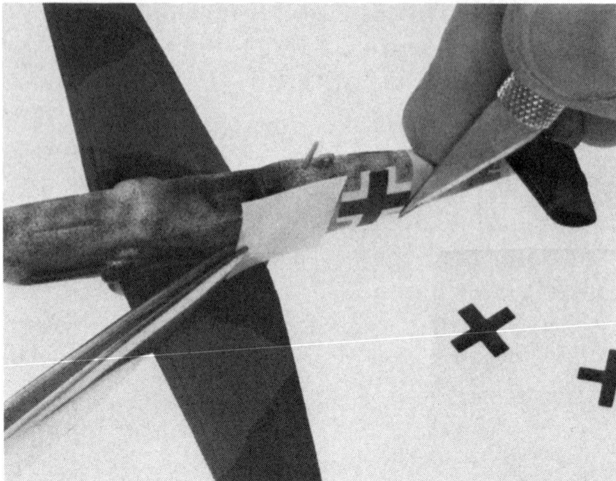

Figure 5-3. Hold the decal with the tip of a hobby knife while the decal's paper backing is pulled away with tweezers.

Figure 5-4. Apply decal-softening fluid beneath and on top of the decal to force the decal to conform to rivet detail.

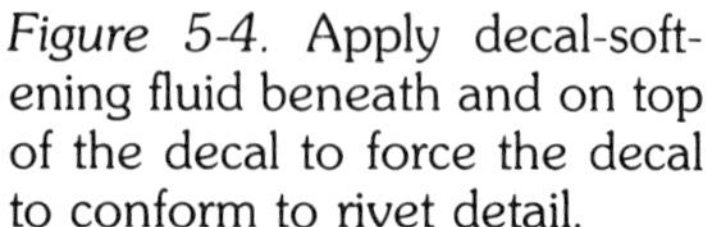

Figure 5-5. Kevin Suddarth used Micro Scale's decals and instructions on his 1/48-scale Otaki P-51D Mustang.

surfaces (the tops of the wings, for example) and let the softener dry for two to six hours. If the decal is hugging tightly to every detail, you can proceed to another set of decals on, for example, the bottom of the wings. Cloudy spots in the decal indicate trapped air; pierce the spot with a pin and apply another coat of the decal softening fluid.

Some areas with sharp curves or details may need as many as six coats of decal softener on top of the decal (waiting between coats for each one to dry) before the decal will conform to every detail on the model's surface. *Never* touch a decal that has been softened with decal softening fluid. The decal will be so soft that it will move like almost-dry paint and, if it does, the decal is ruined and you must remove it. You may be able to skip the use of decal softener with the Scale-Master decals unless a trapped air pocket appears after the decal has dried.

It is best to plan on using four evenings to apply a set of decals: one evening for the top surfaces, one for the bottom surfaces, one for the right of the fuselage, and one for the left of the fuselage. The decals must dry face up to adhere tightly to the model's surface. The actual decal application time will only take an hour or so, but it will take the rest of the evening for the decal softener coats to dry (perhaps even two evenings if several coats of softener are needed).

Finishing the Decals   When the softening fluid on the final decal has dried completely, the model must be scrubbed very lightly with a damp and lint-free paper towel to remove all traces of glue and residue from the decal softening fluids. If you leave these materials on the faces of the decals or on the model, they will turn cloudy or brown and they may even stain the paint. Wipe the model down and let it dry one more day. The final coat of clear paint can then be sprayed over the entire model (except for the clear plastic windows or canopies). The final coat serves three purposes: it protects the decals so they will not be loosened by humidity from the air or from your hands; it helps to smooth the edge of the decal film so the decal appears to be thinner; and it gives both the decals and the paint the same sheen. Even if you are applying a glossy decal to a model that will also remain glossy, there will always be a slight difference between the surface finishes on the decal and on the rest of the model. When you spray both surfaces with the same clear paint, the entire model will have the same reflective quality.

Decal Stripes

Most modelers find it much easier to apply stripes or lines or even checkerboard patterns with decals than with paint. It is almost always easier to move a decal of a stripe into place then to try to mask that same area with either Scotch Magic tape or the masking fluids. There is an incredible assortment of stripe and checkerboard colors and sizes available from decal makers. You can also buy solid color sheets of decals or even

Figure 5-6. Micro Scale offers a variety of stripe and checkerboard decals that are easier to apply than paint.

clear sheets that you can paint to make your own decals. Some modelers even apply camouflage patterns with sharp color separation lines using decals.

You will need at least a half dozen applications of decal softening fluid to cover the width of a wing, for example, or a cowl with a decal. The real secret is to get the decal aligned precisely before the softening fluid starts to work. You usually have about five minutes, after applying the softening fluid, to move the decal around on the model. If you hold the model close to your eye so you can sight down it, you can generally get stripes straighter than you could with a ruler. Double-check the alignment after the fluid has been at work for about ten minutes; you'll still be able to make minor adjustments in the decal without ruining it. If the decal is not straight after about ten minutes, use tweezers to remove it from the model immediately and start over with a fresh decal. If the decal has dried, you can remove it by sticking some Scotch Magic tape over it; the decal will come off with the tape. Any remaining bits of decal can be scrubbed off with a lint-free paper towel dipped in decal softening fluid.

Dry Transfer Markings

Dry transfers are now a common product for artists and draftsmen. Stores that cater to these two professions carry hundreds of different types of lettering, numbers, stripes, and decorative trim in several colors. These products are like decals but they use a special kind of wax, rather than water-soluble glue, to hold them in place. The obvious advantage of dry transfers is that there is no clear film on the model to worry about and, if the transfer is applied properly, it will adhere to any rivet or panel detail without the use of decal softening fluids.

To apply a dry transfer, place the sheet (the side on which the design or letter is printed in reverse) face down on the model and rub lightly over the back of the design with a dull-pointed instrument like the tip of a ballpoint pen. This transfers the marking to the surface of the model. Then lift the clear film away. If the dry transfer is not flush with every surface

Figure 5-7. Decal stripes, shaped to fit the nose of the aircraft, make commercial airliners' paint schemes easy to duplicate.

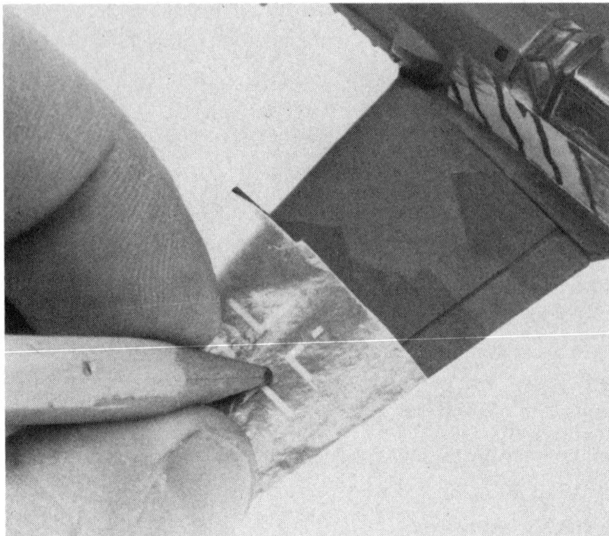

Figure 5-8. Apply dry transfer markings or lettering by rubbing over the backing sheet with a dull-pointed lead pencil.

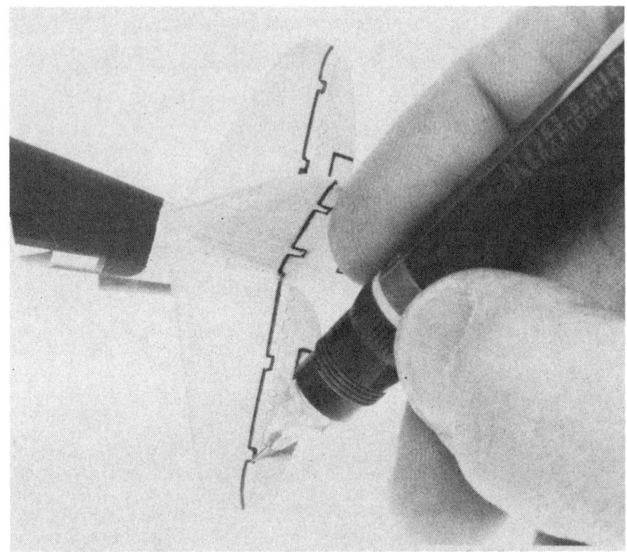

Figure 5-9. Accent shadows along panel or control surface seams with black ink using a drafting pen with a number 00 tip.

detail, dab at it lightly with a soft rubber pencil eraser to push it tightly onto the surface. *Do not* use decal softening fluid with any brand of dry transfer; the fluid will curl the dry transfer into a tight little ball. Most of the clear paints that will not attack decals will not attack dry transfers either, but try your favorite type of clear paint on a sample dry transfer applied to a scrap of plastic to make sure. As with decals, the dry transfer must be protected and blended into the model with clear paint. The dry transfer's waxy "glue" will loosen, in time, if the transfer is not protected.

The dry transfer is rather tricky to apply because you have to put it in exactly the right place the first time. If you rub over the clear backing

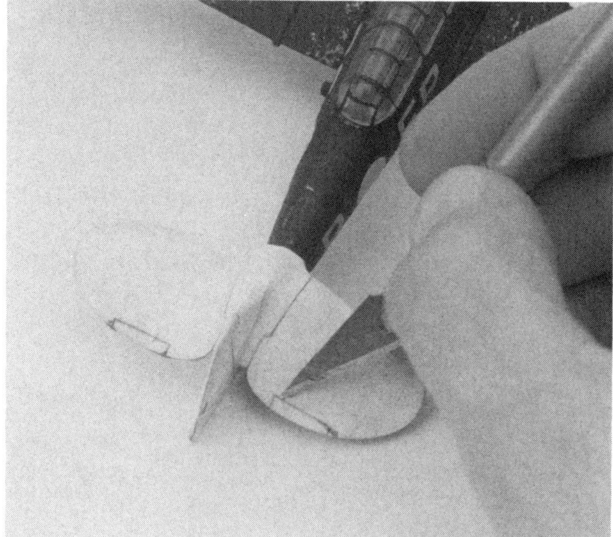

Figure 5-10. Slice gently over the panel lines and control surface lines with a sharp hobby knife.

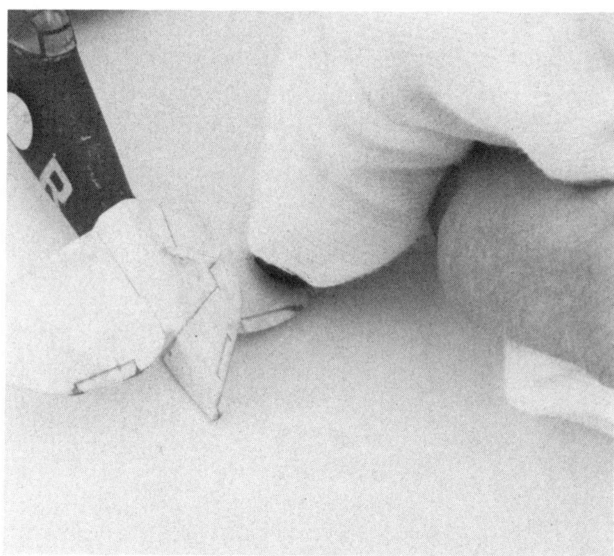

Figure 5-11. Brush black India ink over the knife cuts and wipe the excess ink away before it dries.

and discover the transfer has moved, you'll need to remove the transfer and start again. If you stick some Scotch Magic tape to the transfer and pull, the transfer will come off with the tape.

For some reason, dry transfers are fairly popular with model railroaders so you may find some unusual numbers, letters or markings among the dry transfers sold for that hobby. The markings for some private aircraft and other symbols may only be available as dry transfers. It is possible to make a decal out of a dry transfer by rubbing the transfer onto a sheet of clear decal film. You will not, however, be able to use decal softening fluid on top of the decal—if the fluid you apply to the model *before* applying the decal doesn't make it adhere to the details, you'll just have to remove the decal and try again. With this method you will, at least, be able to move the marking around to get it into the proper position.

Panel Lines and Seams

The hinge lines along the flaps and control surfaces and the panel lines around doors and access panels are far more visible on a real aircraft than on a model. Part of the reason for this is that, on the real aircraft, those really are gaps and they are highlighted with shadows. You can simulate that effect on a model by painting in a shadow or just by adding a thin black line.

There are two acceptable methods for adding these lines: to simply draw them onto the model with either a sharp number 2 lead pencil or a number 00 drafting pen, or to slice the model with a knife and fill in the cut with ink. The drafting pen (even if you use a number 0000 point) makes a line that is really a bit too wide to simulate a shadow. This can be quite realistic, however, on a light-colored surface, particularly after the surface has been weathered a bit with simulated dirt. If regular drafting ink won't work, try using Scalecoat II paint thinned with an equal part of Scalecoat II thinner, or Polly S paint thinned with an equal part of water. Clean the drafting pen as soon as the lines are in place so the paint won't dry inside the pen's orifices. Do not use any of the other brands of paint or they may attack the pen's plastic.

You can achieve a very close to scale simulation of the hairline cracks around flaps and doors by cutting over those lines lightly with a sharp hobby knife. Brush jut a trace of waterproof India ink along the cuts and wipe the ink off immediately with a damp lint-free paper towel. The ink will remain only in the cut lines if you brush over just a few inches of the cuts at a time so the ink does not dry on the surfaces or edges of the panel lines. Use grey or black ink, depending on how pronounced you feel the panel lines should be.

Either technique will be most effective if you use it after the decals are in place but before spraying on the final coat of clear paint. Any flap or panel lines that cross over decals can then be drawn or cut right over the decal. When the ink is dry, the final coat of clear paint can be sprayed over the model.

Chapter 6

The Art of Weathering

THE assembly, painting and decaling of miniature aircraft is a process that demands a great deal of skill and patience. The molding details on most of the model aircraft kits are correct; proper paint colors are available or they can be matched to color chips; photographs of the real aircraft tell you where the paint and decals should be applied. In all, it's a fairly mechanical process. Weathering, however, is something that is far more subtle and much more in the realm of art than the other areas of modeling. You must be an observer of nature and its effects on the real aircraft if you hope to match the effects of age and wear that modelers call weathering. No photograph or painting will give you all the information you need to recreate the appearance of a well-used aircraft in miniature. You alone must judge whether, for example, the exhaust stains should be subdued or exaggerated to gain the most realistic effect on a model. You must also decide whether just flat paint will do for simulating the slight aging effects of oxidation or if you must add white to the paint to prebleach it. Since the whole process of weathering begins on the real aircraft with the factory colors, that's the place for you to begin as well.

Matching the Factory Colors

Aircraft modelers are fortunate to have an incredible selection of research material available to them thanks to the enthusiasm of aircraft historians. You may have heard that the colors reproduced in books can be very far removed from the true color of the aircraft. Even if the artist did capture the color, much will be lost in the printing process. A color chart, for example, can be perfectly correct at the beginning of a press run and, before 10,000 copies are printed, the colors can be off by several shades. You should use color paintings, profiles, postcards, or photographs only as rough guides to the actual colors of any full-size aircraft. The paints for modelers are just as variable, from one batch of paint to another and from one manufacturer to another.

Color chips, actually painted from the correct color formulas, are available for most of the aircraft from World War II right up to the present and for aircraft from many larger countries. If you have the proper color chip you can make an educated decision about whether a pre-mixed paint color is close enough or whether you must mix your own color. You can

Figure 6-1. Notice the chipped and worn paint on this early WWII-era FM2 Wildcat. *Photo courtesy U.S. Navy.*

also decide if one of the pre-mixed colors might just be the color you want *when that color had been exposed to the bleaching effects of sun, rain and wind.* You can even use the color chips to determine just which blue, for instance, a painter might be indicating in the box art of your favorite aircraft.

The majority of the colors used by American armed forces are available as color chips in the publication *Federal Standard No.595a Colors, Volume I.* This publication is currently $2.25 from The Specifications Activity, Printed Materials Supply Division, Building 197, National Weapons Plant, Washington, DC 20407. Only the color chips and their FS numbers are given. The FS-series numbers appear in many publications dealing with full-size aircraft and are included in some aircraft model kits and with some decal sheets. Color chips for German aircraft colors appear in *Modelers Luftwaffe Painting Guide with Color Chart,* an 88-page book from Kookabura Publications (see the address under "Publications"). The books *Japanese Naval Air Force Camouflage and Markings, WWII,* and *Japanese Army Air Force Camouflage and Markings, WWII,* by Don Thorpe (Aero Publishers), refer to Munsell color chips. These chips are a standard guide to colors and they are available through most artists and printing supply stores. You may be able to locate paint references to this color standard in publications on the full-size aircraft from other countries in your local public library. A list of just a few of the publishers and mail order dealers in aircraft literature are included in the Sources section of this book.

Simulating Bare Aluminum

With the exception of some World War II fighters, a few modern private aircraft, and the aircraft of the thirties, all the miniatures you'll build will be replicas of aircraft that had some type of aluminum alloy skin. You can get around the need to simulate the aluminum by selecting a prototype that was painted, but even then you may want to reproduce weathering effects that expose the aluminum beneath chipped and peeling paint. The majority of the paints that are labeled "aluminum" look like paint regardless of what you do to them. There are a number of full-size aircraft that have their aluminum skins painted an aluminum color and those are certainly the ones to pick if you prefer the easy way out. There are several alternatives to this, such as using special paints that contain metal so you can actually polish them like real aluminum, applying thin aluminum foil to the aircraft, or plating it (like some of Testor's kits).

Airbrushing an Aluminum Finish You really must apply any aluminum color or real aluminum paint with an airbrush if you hope to get the model to look like the real thing. The paint must be applied with a relatively low air pressure so it flows just a bit to give a perfectly smooth texture. If the paint is too wet, the surface will puddle with microscopic flecks of metal.

If you look closely at almost any real aircraft that has an aluminum skin, you'll discover two things: each of the panels has a slightly different color than the others, and the metal really does have a bit of a shine.

Use Scotch Magic tape to divide the model into about three areas to simulate the patchwork colors on the real aircraft. You will paint about one-third of the panels with aluminum out of the bottle, about one-third of them with a slightly darker shade (obtained by mixing two or three drops of dark blue in the paint), and about one-third with a slightly lighter shade (obtained by mixing two or three drops of white in the paint). It's best to start by spraying the entire model with paint straight from the bottle. When that is dry, mask off two-thirds of the panels with tape and spray the visible one-third with the darker color. When that color dries, cover it with Magic tape and remove the Magic tape from a different one-third of the panels so they can be sprayed with the lighter shade. Select the panels in a random pattern to duplicate the appearance of the panels on the real aircraft. If you're using aluminum-colored paint, you can simulate some of the shine by spraying the model with clear gloss (rather than clear flat) paint after the decals are in place.

The paints containing real metal that can be polished seem to be difficult to obtain but the search might be worth your trouble. Look for either Spray-N-Plate or Liqu-A-Plate in bottles. Both are available in light and dark shades so you don't have to mix in the drops of blue or white paint unless you want to. These paints are applied with an airbrush as just described for aluminum-colored paints, masking the model between colors to obtain that random array of varied panel colors. When the paint is completely dry, it can actually be polished with a soft rag and just a bit of very mild polish like Blue Magic or plain toothpaste. The Liqu-A-Plate paints should be allowed to dry for about a *month* before applying decals and a final coat of clear gloss paint.

Be sure to test any brand of clear gloss paint on a sample of plastic painted with the real metal aluminum paint; some brands of clear gloss oxidize the metal to a flat, dark shade. The aluminum paints will make scratches and flaws in the model stand out, far more than colored paints would. You can use the Brasso brand household polish to smooth any deep scratches in the plastic before applying the paint.

Using Real Aluminum   It is possible to completely cover a model aircraft with genuine aluminum foil. The thinnest available household cooking foil will work fairly well, but you may be able to find some that is even thinner in a hobby shop that specializes in plastic model aircraft kits. The foil can be glued to the surface of the model with one of the adhesives that are sticky when dry, like Micro Scale's Micro Metal Foil Adhesive. Before using *any* of these glues, be sure to test it on a leftover piece of plastic sprue from the aircraft kit you are working on; some of these glues will dissolve the plastic.

Apply the glue, let it dry until its surface is tacky, then apply the aluminum foil in panels about the size of a group of half-dozen of the real aircraft's panels. The real aircraft are covered in hundreds of panels; a few dozen will capture the effect nicely on a model. Press the foil over the details on the model's surface with your fingertip. The foil should remain in place for about a week before you apply decals and a protective coating of clear flat paint. The foil technique is most effective on larger models in the 1/32-scale range.

Aluminum Plating   If you're really serious about building bare aluminum models, you might want to use the type of plating process Testor's does for some of their 1/48-scale kits. You may be able to find a shop that will vacuum-plate plastic by looking under "Plating" in the telephone book's Yellow Pages. The parts should be plated while still attached to their sprues. The plater will undoubtedly have a minimum charge and it may be in the $50 to $100 range so it's wise to plate several models at the same time. Before you do, build at least two of Testor's plated kits to see if you really do like the effect.

Testor's has roughened some panels in the molds to produce that

Figure 6-2. Almost every aluminum panel on this F-104A is a slightly different shade of metal. *Photo courtesy U.S. Air Force.*

Figure 6-3. These surface panels have been sprayed different shades of Spray-N-Plate to simulate the patchwork appearance of full-size modern jets.

Figure 6-4. Lloyd Jones painted this Dragon Model Works 1/72-scale vacuum-formed Bristol T.188 with Spray-N-Plate aluminum.

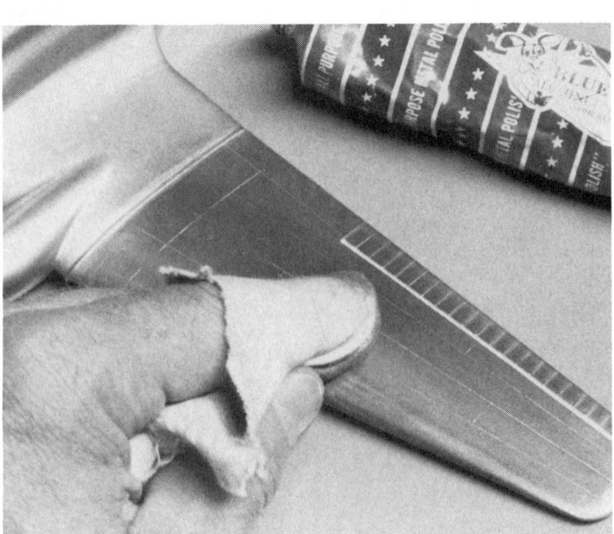

Figure 6-5. The aluminum metal dust in the Spray-N-Plate allows the model to be polished, when the paint is dry, so the surface looks exactly like aluminum.

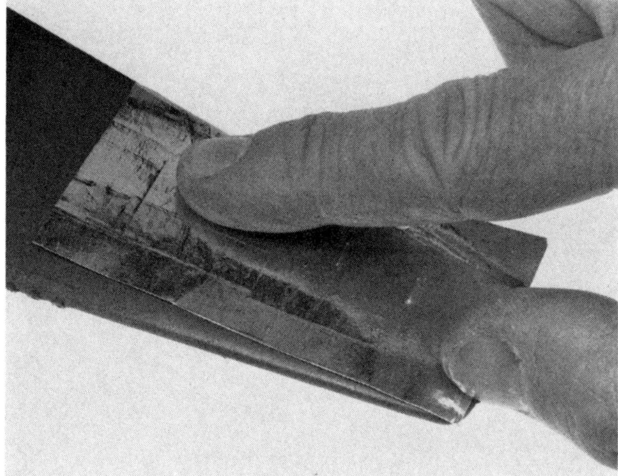

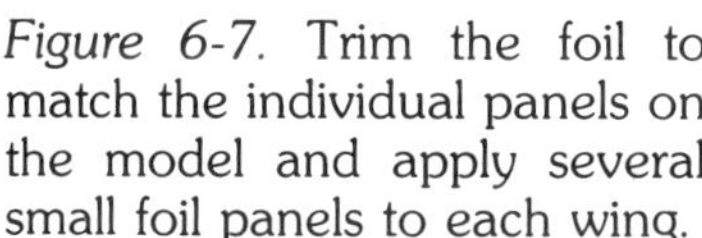

Figure 6-6. Foil can be used, with Micro Scale's Micro Metal Foil Adhesive, to simulate aluminum-skinned aircraft.

Figure 6-7. Trim the foil to match the individual panels on the model and apply several small foil panels to each wing.

multi-colored panel effect. You can do something similar to your kits by brushing some liquid cement for plastics over a random number of panels *before* the parts are plated. You can highlight the effect by brushing a wash of about 19 parts clear gloss and 1 part dark blue or white paint over a random number of panels after they have been plated. The wash will give the panels an off-color appearance similar to what you can achieve by mixing a touch of color with aluminum-color paint. It might be possible to apply the "wash" with an airbrush but there's a very good chance that Magic tape or even masking fluid might lift or damage some of the plating.

Plating can be one of the most effective techniques if you are careful to paint any visible bare plastic with silver or aluminum paint. The model can then be weathered slightly with several overall "washes" of 1 part flat black or white paint with about 19 parts or more of clear gloss. Do not

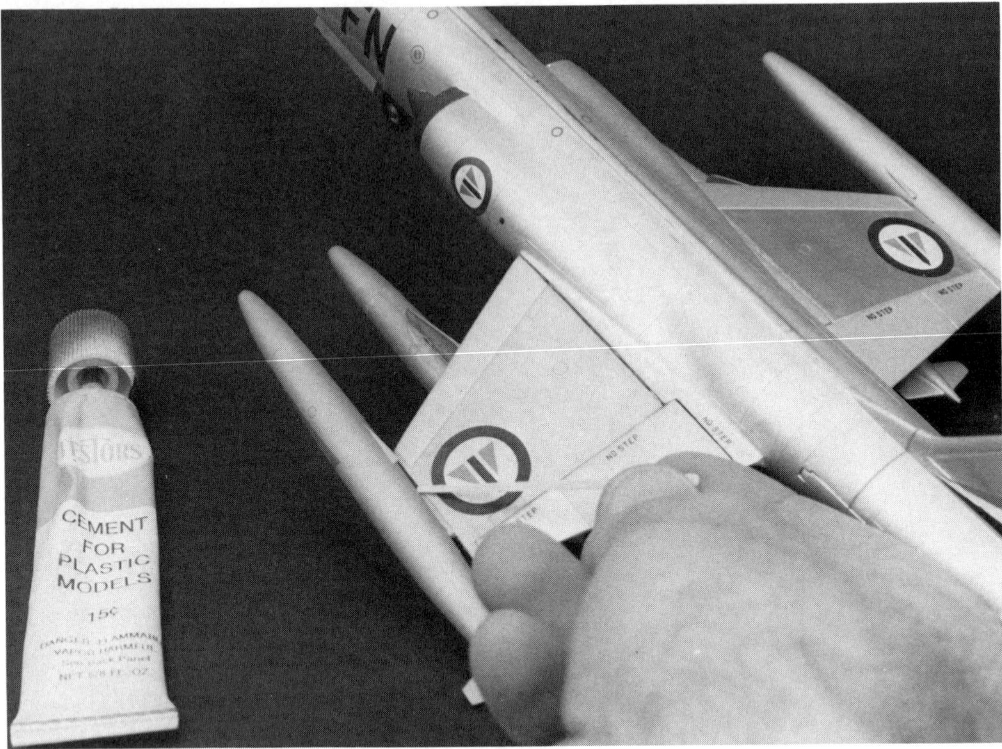

Figure 6-8. The plated surfaces of some of the Testor's kits, like this F-104A, produce an incredibly realistic simulation of bare aluminum. The plated parts can be assembled with plastic cement if the plating is scraped from the joints.

attempt to weather a plated model with the usual "wash" of thinner and paint as the thinner may attack the clear coating that holds the plating to the model's surface.

The Aging Process

A real aircraft begins to change its appearance the moment it leaves the production line. The movement of the machine through the air, the maintenance work it receives, and the effects of age and weather provide a constantly-changing pattern on the aircraft. It would be fascinating, indeed, if a film maker could prepare a 5-minute long motion picture on the aging process of an aircraft over a 24-month period like those films of clouds in action over a 24-hour period. You would see how the bright and even colors fade and mottle as flights through rain and hail and sand chip away at the paint while the sun bleaches and dulls the colors. Mechanics dribble fuel and oil and other fluids around the cockpit while the engine itself provides oil leaks and exhaust stains. The paint wears down to the bare metal where the endless parade of pilots step on the wings or open cockpits and hatches. From time to time, a bright fresh area appears where the maintenance crews replace or repaint a panel. Those effects are the ones you want to achieve with your model but, unlike the real thing, you're going to provide a "stop-action" three-dimensional portrait of the aircraft at one particular point in its life.

One of the most interesting aircraft displays I have ever seen depicted a P-38 fighter in three different stages of aging using three different models: bright and neat as it rolled off the production line, slightly worn after about six months of service, and very faded with great chunks of bare aluminum visible where the paint had chipped, a shiny new rudder flap to replace one that had been lost in battle, new guns and new radar, and a few shiny aluminum patches over damaged areas. This scene of the same aircraft as it traveled through time was an incredible sight.

The simulation of the aging process on a miniature aircraft starts with the first coat of paint. You must decide right then how much wear or weathering you will want to display on the finished model. Weathering on a miniature starts from the inside and works it way out, just the opposite of how the effects are created in real life. If your model is going to be an aluminum aircraft that has been painted then you may want to paint the model aluminum so you can duplicate the chipped paint of the prototype. There is no better way to simulate chipped paint that reveals an aluminum "skin" than to actually chip the paint to reveal a *painted* aluminum "skin". Most full-size aircraft receive a coat of green-yellow zinc chromate primer before they receive any color coats; if you are going to depict chipped paint, then you should cover the aluminum with a primer coat of zinc chromate. If the real aircraft was cloth, you may want to cut away an area and install a panel of .010-inch thin plastic that has been "torn" with a hobby knife to simulate a rip in the cloth covering.

How to Chip Paint

The most effective method of simulating chipped paint is to chip the paint. The characteristics of paint for models are such, however, that the paint is not supposed to chip so you'll have to go out of your way to do it. The problem is a bit more complex than it might seem because you want to be able to control very precisely just where the paint will chip and where it will remain secure.

The pre-chipping process begins with that first coat of aluminum paint. After weathering there should only be very small areas of aluminum showing through so there's no need to use the paints that actually have metal in them. Use the aluminum color paints from the same manufacturer as the paints you will use for the other colors. When the aluminum has dried for a day, carefully brush on small patches of liquid floor wax using a number 00 brush to keep the patches as small as possible. Let the wax dry, then spray on the zinc chromate-color (if the aircraft you are modeling did have that color primer coat) and allow it to dry. The patches of wax should be visible as slight humps in the primer color if you hold the model so light reflects off the paint surface. You may find it impossible to apply paint over the wax with a paintbrush—I can only recommend this method of weathering if you can apply the paint with aerosol cans or with an airbrush. When the zinc chromate color has dried for a day, brush on more liquid floor wax in precisely the same places as the first patches but make these just a bit larger in area. You can apply a few more patches of the wax in areas where you want to simulate paint that has only chipped down to the zinc chromate color.

Apply the final color coats and, when they are dry, apply the clear gloss for the decals and the decals themselves. Do not apply the final protective coat of clear paint, however. The paint can now be chipped by simply pressing masking tape or Scotch Magic tape onto the surface over those wax spots and lifting the tape. The paint will peel off with the tape leaving a chipped area that shows the aluminum color surrounded by a ragged ring of the zinc chromate primer. Do not apply the tape to any of the decals; scrape those areas of paint and decal away with a tip of a hobby knife. When you have made all the chipped paint areas you need to duplicate a real aircraft, gently wipe away any excess wax with rubbing alcohol. Then apply the final coat of clear flat paint.

I would suggest you practice this method on an old model to get the feeling of how the technique works. It takes only a very few, very small chips to create the proper effect.

Faded Paint Effects

The sun bleaches paint with a chemical reaction that takes place in the paint itself. You cannot add on this color like the weathering effects of washed-down dirt or exhaust stains. Do not, then, attempt to duplicate

Figure 6-9. Duplicate chipped paint by using tape to peel paint away from spots of wax.

faded paint by covering a color coat with a "wash" of light grey paint or thinner. This method simulates, at best, the look of light-colored soil washed over the aircraft by rain.

The basic aircraft colors must be mixed with small amounts of white paint so that each color appears to be as faded as the next. Experiment by adding about 10-percent white paint to partially-filled bottles of each color, then apply the color to a scrap of cardboard or plastic and let it dry. Look at the color under the light where the model will be displayed to determine if you have the right shade for each of the aircraft's colors. Paint, especially "faded" paint, will look quite different under natural sunlight, natural shade, and fluorescent or incandescent lighting. What looks nicely faded on your workbench may look like pastel-colored house paint on the display shelf. You may have to mix as much as 30 to 40-percent white paint with each color to achieve the look of some World War II warplanes' colors. When you are satisfied, label the bottle with the color mixing formula and the date so you can mix more paint if you need it.

You can simulate similar fading on the decals by rubbing them very lightly with the finest grade of steel wool. Some areas of the decals should be rubbed right through so the paint is visible from beneath them.

Simulating Worn Paint

An additional type of weathering that must be simulated if you expect the model to look like the real thing is worn or weather-scoured paint. The worn and weather-scoured look must be "applied" first. If you painted the aircraft with aluminum-colored paint beneath the color coats, you can actually wear away the paint with fine steel wool or number 600 wet-or-dry sandpaper dipped frequently in water. Work gently because this, like all weathering effects, is something that is very easy to overdo. Scrub the paint away so a few of the rivets show through as aluminum, but don't be too discouraged if you go all the way through to the bare plastic—the way to fix it is described below.

Look very carefully at photos of the real aircraft to determine which areas wear the most. The leading edges of the wings, rudder and stabilizer will certainly receive a lot of wear as will the tops of the wings (on a fighter) where the pilot steps into the cockpit. Wear will also occur near doors, hatches, and other access areas where the mechanics must reach for maintenance or to load bombs or bullets.

When you're reasonably satisfied with your wear patterns, turn your attention to finer details. Dip the tip of your finger, wrapped tightly in a lint-free paper towel, into some Rub'n Buff silver-colored paste. Rub off the excess paste on a scrap of paper. Very gently touch the remaining paste to the wear areas to cover any exposed plastic and to impart a slightly different shade to random areas of rivet heads and panel seams.

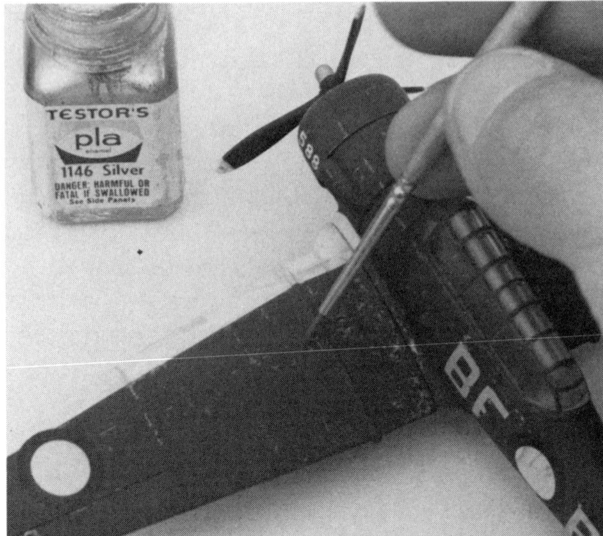

Figure 6-10. Dry brush aluminum paint on the tops of rivets and seams to simulate colored paint worn through to the metal.

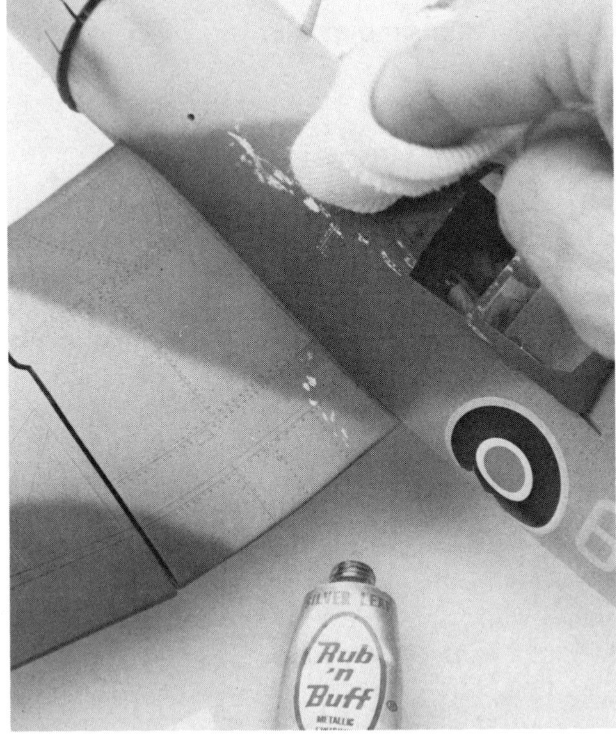

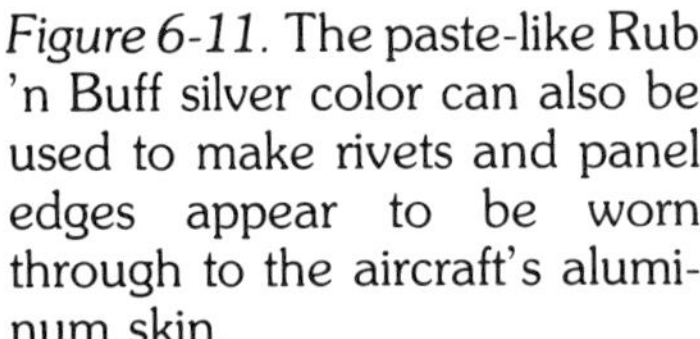

Figure 6-11. The paste-like Rub 'n Buff silver color can also be used to make rivets and panel edges appear to be worn through to the aircraft's aluminum skin.

Rub 'n Buff is sold by hardware and craft supply stores for "antiquing" furniture and sculpture.

You could also dry brush silver or aluminum paint on the small details to simulate paint worn through to the metal. Dry brushing is a technique that uses just enough paint to stick to the longest bristle tips of the brush. Dip the brush only 1/16 inch into the paint and squeeze off most of the paint on a scrap of paper so the brush is almost dry. Brush very lightly on the top of rivets and seams to simulate worn paint.

Simulating Dirt and Stains

There are very few external stains on an aircraft. Rust and dirt accumulate quickly on machines that stay on the ground but aircraft are not generally exposed to such effects. There are exceptions to this rule, including warplanes that land on dirt runways or that are housed in revetments with earthen banks on three sides. Most of the external stains on a real aircraft are the result of smoking exhaust pipes, smoking machine guns, fuel leaks, or oil leaks and spills.

In any case, the stains are very light and translucent, even when an exhaust pipe trails its soot over a blue cowl. Do not use pure black paint for exhaust or gunpowder stains; a mixture of about half black and half brown is close to the real color. The residue that accumulates in your paintbrush or airbrush washing solvent is probably just about the right color when reduced to a "wash" of nine or more parts thinner to one part paint. Apply very light and thin coats, allowing each application to dry so you can see if you have achieved the desired effect. The color will be much darker after it has dried so use this method to avoid applying too much of the stain.

If you have mastered the use of the airbrush, adjust the air pressure to about 15 psi and decrease the paint flow so you can spray a pencil-thin line or patch. If you are using a brush, use a combination of a dabbing and a streaking action so the exhaust or gunpowder stains won't look like black stripes. Use a fine-pore sponge to dab on stains near cockpit handles and other access areas where dirty hands might have blackened the area.

Simulating Wood and Cloth

There is a surprising amount of wood in aircraft built prior to World War II. Wooden propellors, wooden airframes (the aircraft's interior structure) and even wooden wings were used on a number of full-size aircraft. The wood is not visible, even as wood grain texture, when reduced to the scale of most model aircraft. The only exceptions might be areas of a model that are meant to simulate damage from battle or a crash. In these instances, you can use real wood that's available from hobby shops that specialize in flying model aircraft.

The only visible wood on most aircraft models should be the propellor on World War I, between-the-wars, and some private aircraft. Often, real wood propellors are merely painted with clear varnish or shellac so the wood grain shows through. On a model, the wood grain can be effectively simulated by painting the propellor a light beige with perhaps just a touch of yellow. When the beige is dry, medium or dark brown paint is dry brushed over it to duplicate the dark grain effect of real wood. If you brush very lightly over the propellor, the brush will leave single streaks

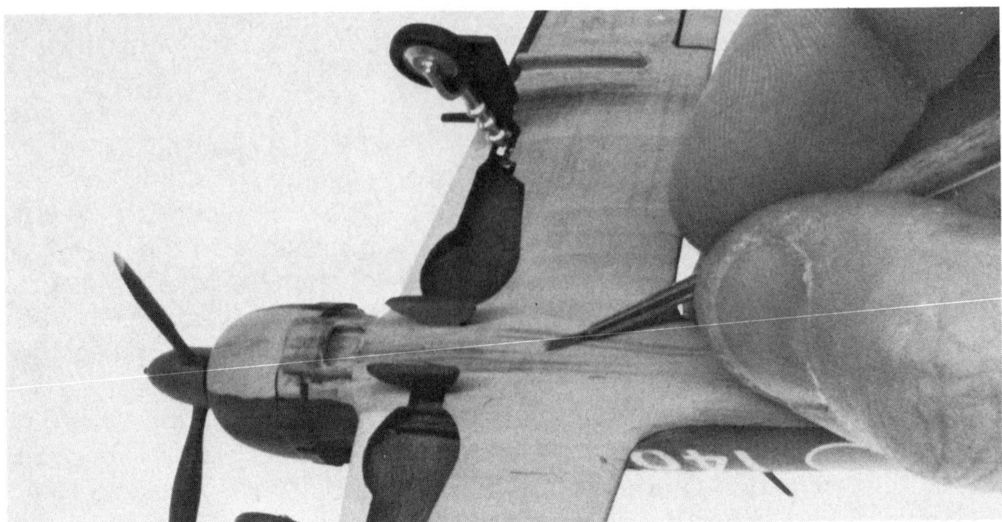

Figure 6-12. Dan Wilson used a wash of dark brown paint and clear paint to apply the exhaust and gunpowder stains to his Revell Ki61 "Tony" conversion.

of brown. The technique requires a bit of practice but it can be most useful whenever a streaked finish is required.

The only time that cloth would be visible on a model aircraft would be when the aircraft has been damaged by bullets or by a crash so the cloth is torn. You can use very thin silk or nylon on a 1/32-scale aircraft, but Evergreen's .010-inch thick plastic sheet is more effective in the smaller scales. The plastic can be cut in a starburst pattern to simulate the tear.

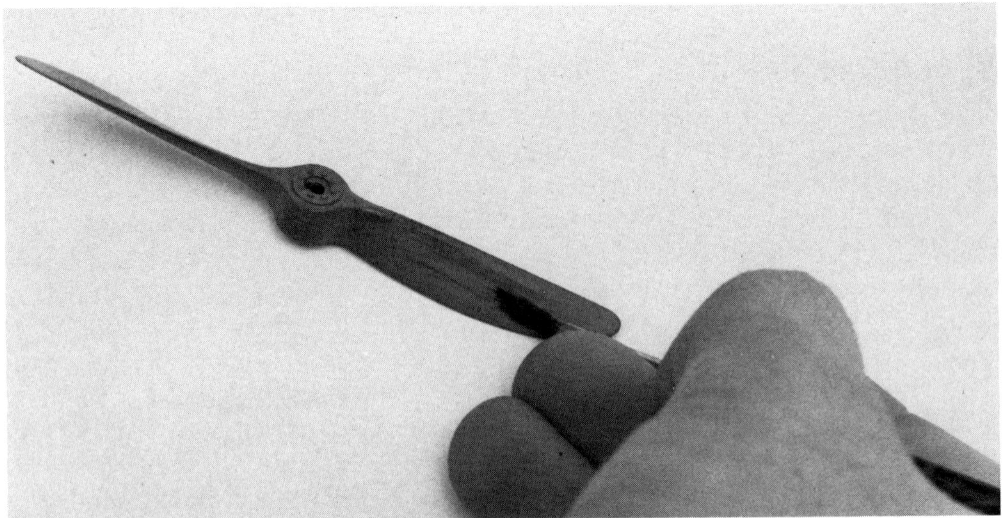

Figure 6-13. Dry brush dark brown over a base coat of beige to simulate the wood grain of a varnished wooden propellor.

The tips of the star are then curled at random to simulate the curled appearance of painted cloth that has been torn. A plastic panel with the "tear" can simply be glued in place over the model's surface before the model is painted and the edges of the .010 inch thick plastic smoothed with one of the filler putties.

Battle Damage

A great many modelers enjoy simulating the bullet holes and the torn surfaces of warplanes that have suffered battle damage. These effects are interesting to simulate but many models are damaged so badly that the aircraft would never fly. That's just fine if you're building a diorama of a crash scene or an aircraft scrap scene. If you are attempting to create a replica of a warplane that might have been able to land with the damage you are simulating, then that damage must be very subtle indeed.

The extensive battle damage that exposes the aircraft's inner structure must be built into the model from the start. The Plastruct line of ABS plastic structural shapes includes several 1/16 inch high I, H, and L shapes that can be most effective in simulating the structure of an aircraft. The books and magazines that describe the real aircraft often have cut-away views of the airframe structure that you can use as a reference to simulate the ribs and spars and braces that would be visible if the aircraft's skin were torn away. The aircraft's skin can be simulated with either .010 inch thick plastic sheet or with aluminum foil cut and ripped to match photographs of battle damage on the full-size aircraft. The techniques for simulating wear and weathering can also be used around any ripped or torn outer panels.

Figure 6-14. Small bits of wire and .010 inch thick Evergreen sheet plastic can be used to duplicate severe battle damage.

Figure 6-15. The helicopters in Tom Leonard's diorama have been damaged so severely that they are relegated to a scrap or spare part storage yard.

Most battle damage is slight and it can be simulated after the model is painted and after the decals are in place but before that final coat of clear flat paint is applied. To simulate bullet holes, heat the tip of a straight pin over a candle flame. Hold the pin with pliers and press it into the surface of the aircraft to make the bullet hole. A small ridge of plastic will surround the hole but this can be touched with aluminum paint or Rub 'n Buff silver-colored paste so it looks like the edge of a real bullet hole. Be sure to drag the heated pin across the surface in some places to simulate holes from bullets that entered the surface at an angle—far too many modelers duplicate only round bullet holes. The edges of each of the holes should be aluminum with just a single dot of black paint (applied with the tip of a pin) in the center of the simulated bullet holes.

If the bullet holes are in the area of the engines, you may want to simulate an engine fire by streaking a "wash" of dark brown from the engine to the edges of the panel lines that indicate the removable cowl and access panels. Bullet holes in a canopy must be formed with a small drill bit. Cracks can be simulated by scribing the clear plastic surface with a sharp hobby knife.

Chapter 7

Details

CONTEMPORARY model kits include almost every detail you could want on a miniature aircraft. The standards of die-making have increased considerably in the last decade or so. Even the snap-together plastic model kits include more authentic shapes and more true-to-scale surface details. The details on some of the 1/48 and 1/32-scale models extend right down to the cockpit floor and into the engine bay and landing gear interiors. Most modelers are content to merely finish what is supplied in the kit with correct paint and, perhaps, weathering effects. I would suggest that you spend most of your efforts learning to build the stock kit correctly with filler putty and a perfect paint and decal finish. You cannot hide poor assembly quality by trying to distract the viewer's eye to a single well-detailed area of the model. The super details you'll find in this chapter will only be effective if the overall impression of the model is so strikingly realistic that the viewer *expects* to find more detail in a closer look at the model.

The Scrap Box

Every model building enthusiast must be a bit of a pack rat because each of us has a hoard of miscellaneous bits and pieces that are kept in a scrap box. Anything that looks tiny enough to be suitable for use on a model should be put in the scrap box for possible use later on. Ball-headed shirt pins from new shirts, bits of wire or plastic insulation from telephone installations, paper clips of all sizes, scraps of foil and plastic, and other such materials are all suitable for the scrap box. Many kits include optional parts that certainly belong in a scrap box. If you choose to build a model with its landing gear folded, be sure to save the leftover landing gear. The scrap box will be your primary source of the small bits and pieces that are used to simulate the details of a cockpit interior, engine bay or landing gear bay.

Special Tools

There are a few tools that you may want to purchase so you can add superdetails to your model aircraft. These include a pin vise for drilling holes, a jeweler's saw for trimming working flaps, and needle-nosed pliers

Figure 7-1. To add a superdetail to this Revell 1/28-scale SPAD XIII, drill out the tips of the guns with a pin vise.

with diagonal cutters for bending and cutting wire. You may also want to purchase a vacuum-forming machine, like the Formicator shown in Chapter 8 so you can mold cowls, flaps, and canopies from plastic that is closer to scale-thickness aluminum or plastic. Tools like the adjustable-head Panavise with its perfectly flat surface plate make it a bit easier to cut a kit's parts into smaller panels and assemble them more precisely. A Dremel electric motor tool can be most helpful in grinding down the inside of some plastic panels to make them closer to scale thickness, or for cutting and trimming other plastic details.

Making Rivets and Seams

When you file or sand the filler putty in a seam flush with the surface of the model, you cannot avoid removing some of the surface details, like rivets and panel lines. You can replace those rivets, or create rivets for vacuum-formed plastic parts or kits, by using the simple method illustrated here.

Figure 7-2. Use a pair of needle-nosed pliers to push a pin into the surface of the model to form a new rivet.

Figure 7-3. Cross-sectional views of the two steps for making new rivets.

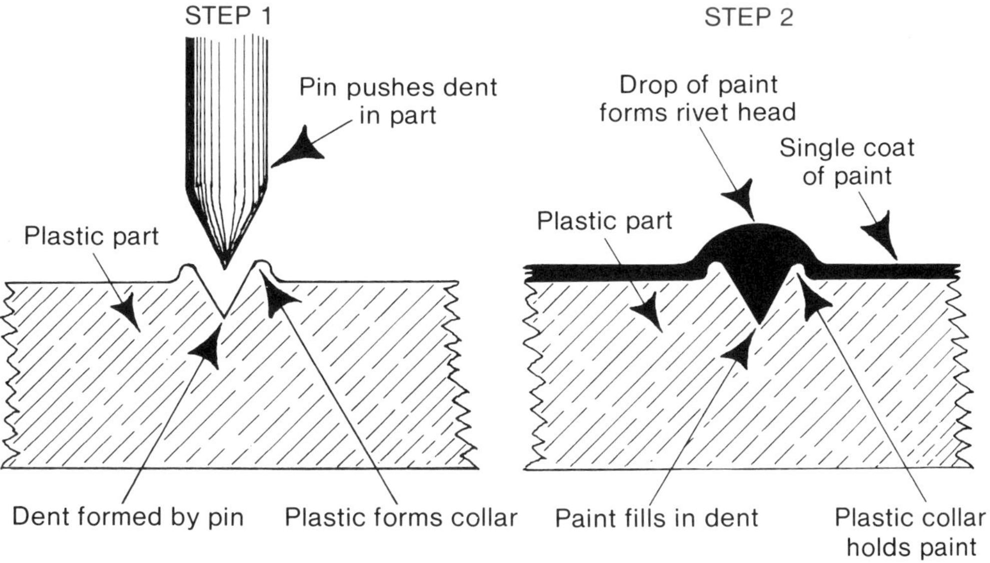

A common straight pin is pushed lightly into the surface of the plastic. It is not necessary to heat the pin unless you need to form a rivet that is more than about 1/32 inch in diameter. The plastic that was in the hole will be forced out to the sides in a mushroom shape. It takes very little pressure to make the entire mushroom, not just the pinhole, the diameter of a scale rivet. The "missing" portion of the rivet's head is formed with a small drop of paint, applied with the tip of another pin. The paint will fill the hole created by the pin to complete the rivet shape. It may be necessary to add another pinpoint of paint, after the first one dries, to completely fill the hole—just don't add so much that the paint flows down the sides of the mushroom around the pinhole.

This same technique can be used to create *raised* panel lines, but a hobby knife is substituted for the pin. With the knife, lightly cut the panel line you want to be raised. Then fill in the cut with paint applied with a ruling pen or a number 00 paintbrush. The paint will form the raised panel line. If you want a recessed panel line, cut a bit deeper with the knife,

Figure 7-4. The cables on 1/72-scale aircraft are as fine as human hairs. They can be made by stretching plastic sprues.

sand the "mushroom" on either side of the cut flush with the surface and run the knife back down the line to clean it out.

Making Cables and Wires

You can create your own hair-size wisps of plastic sprue to be used for radio antennae, for rigging on World War I-era aircraft, or for the cables and lines around an engine or landing gear.

Break off a six-inch piece of straight leftover sprue (the leftover round trees or plastic scraps that the kit parts are attached to). Use a piece that has no elbows or tee-joints in it with at least three inches of perfectly straight plastic. Hold the plastic over a candle flame so the heat from the flame (but not the flame itself) reaches the plastic. When you first notice the plastic beginning to sag, remove it from the flame and pull it gently from both ends. The heat-softened sprue will stretch into a string. The thickness of that string of plastic depends on how hot the plastic is and how rapidly you stretch it. If you pull quickly, the plastic will be very thin; if you pull slowly, the plastic will be fairly thick. With practice you'll be able to stretch sprues into thin threads of plastic anywhere from about .010 inches to .080 inches in diameter. The stretched sprue will be a constant diameter for as much as six inches of its length once you've mastered the technique.

Make the holes for installing cables or antenna wires by depressing the surface of the model with the tip of a pin or needle that has been

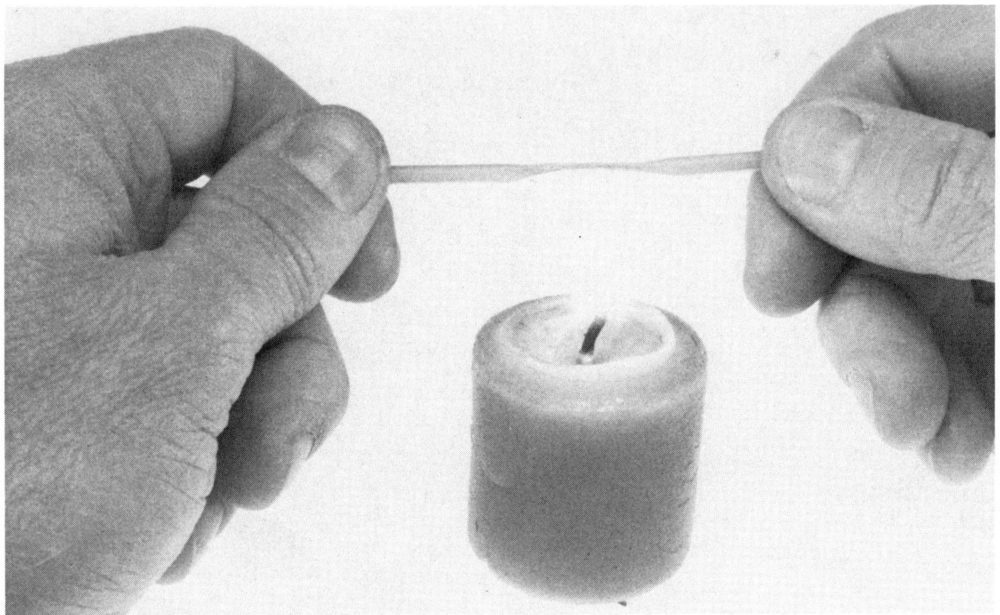

Figure 7-5. Heat a scrap of sprue over a candle flame until it softens. Pull the ends of the sprue to stretch it.

Figure 7-6. Make a small dent with a heated pin; the dent will hold the sprue in place.

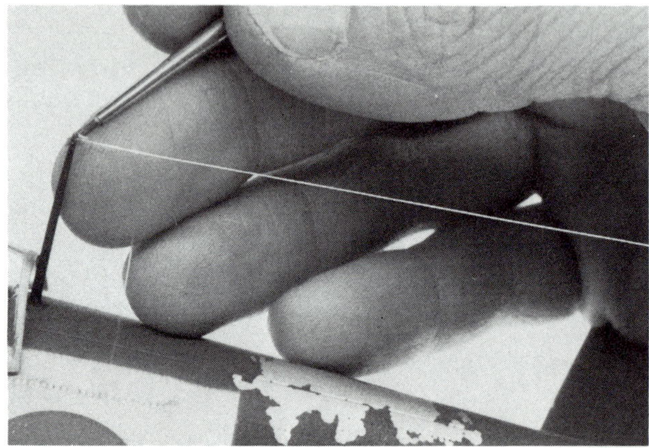

Figure 7-7. Use a drop of five-minute epoxy to hold the stretched sprue to the painted plastic radio aerial.

Figure 7-8. Some antennae have a second vertical wire. Use a stretched sprue and attach it with five-minute epoxy.

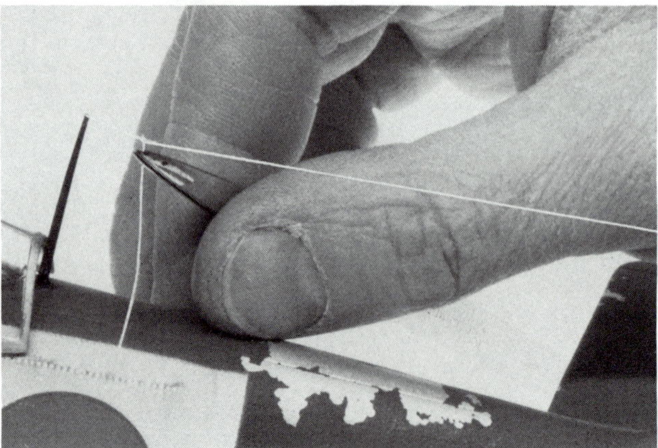

heated over a flame. Attach the stretched sprue to the model with a drop of five-minute epoxy.

Some modelers prefer to stretch the clear plastic leftover from the canopy-molding process to make cables. The different grades of plastic used by kit manufacturers will vary in their reactions to heat. In fact, different colors of plastic from the same kit manufacturer can have dissimilar characteristics. You may find that one type of plastic is easier to work with than others, so experiment with several brands if the sprue-stretching technique seems difficult to learn.

Small diameter linen line intended for sailing ship rigging makes perfect bracing cable for 1/48-scale or larger aircraft models. Paint the line silver or gray after it is in place.

Canopies and Windows

The canopies and windows are the parts of a model aircraft that are the most noticeable when you begin to study the model closely. Unfortunately, these are also the most out-of-scale parts in most plastic aircraft kits, although the problem is not quite so great with 1/32-scale kits. The clear parts in most kits are made about ten times as thick as they should be so the parts will be strong enough to be ejected from the molding machines. A few of the most recent kits have canopies that are very close to scale thickness.

Figure 7-9. Linen line for model sailing ship rigging can be used as bracing cable for 1/48-scale or larger aircraft models.

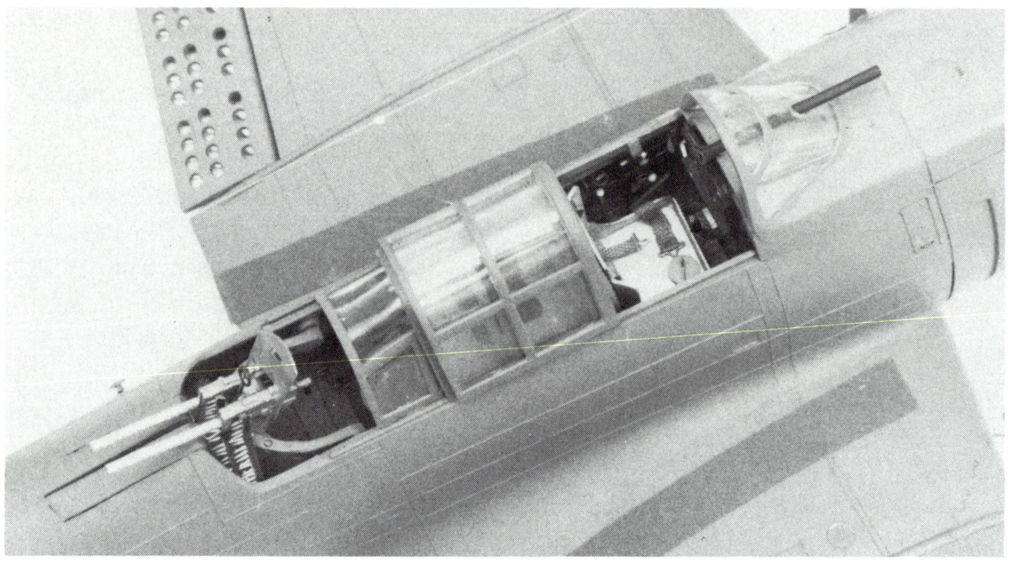

Figure 7-10. This canopy has been vacuum-formed to be the appropriate thickness.

You can mold a clear plastic duplicate of the canopy that came with the kit if you purchase a vacuum-molding machine like the wooden Formicator shown in Chapter 8. If you don't want to invest in your own vacuum-forming machine, you may find a hobby shop that specializes in model aircraft and armored vehicles that will do the work for you. The vacuum-forming machine is a simple tool: it merely draws a sheet of heated plastic tightly over the pattern that is placed in the machine. When you mold a canopy, the shape of the canopy will be molded in the center of a sheet of .010 or .020 inch thick clear acetate or styrene plastic. You must then trim the canopy from the sheet, paint the frame, and glue it in place. The machine can also be used to mold thinner duplicates of engine cowls, control flaps, landing gear flaps or access panels. The thin edges of the vacuum-molded parts add incredible realism to a miniature aircraft.

Figure 7-11 (top). The cockpit of Dennis Nowicki's 1/72-scale Hasegawa P-47D has been detailed with controls, instruments, a radio and seat belts.

Figure 7-12 (middle). Most of the details in this Revell F4u1D "Corsair" cockpit are typical of those in 1/32-scale kits.

Figure 7-13 (bottom). Jerry Crandell carried the cockpit detail out to the stabilizer by positioning the detailed replica of a 1/32-scale pilot's parachute and straps where everyone could see it.

Figure 7-14. The cockpits of jet aircraft include an incredible array of belts, cables and other details.

Cockpit Interiors

If you have finished the exterior surfaces of the model so they capture the appearance of the real aircraft, viewers (including your friends and contest judges) will want to look more closely at the model to see other details. The first place most folks look is inside the cockpit. Almost all 1/72-scale and larger kits include some type of cockpit detail. It is almost impossible to add cockpit detail after the model is completed, because once the fuselage halves are cemented together the cockpit is almost inaccessible.

Most kits include molded-in dashboard instruments and gauges as well as some type of control or radio console. Paint these parts to match the specifications shown on the instruction sheets or in books describing the real aircraft. If you just touch the faces of the panels with a paper towel dipped in silver Rub 'n Buff, the metallic color will accent the rims of the dashboard gauges and the knobs on the control levers. Apply a single drop of clear glossy paint to each of the instrument faces to give them the shine of clear glass. Some firms, like Waldron Model Products, offer superdetail kits for 1/72, 1/48 and 1/32-scale aircraft miniatures. Waldron has an extensive line of dashboards, radios, controls and even tiny etched-metal safety belts to duplicate nearly all the visible details in aircraft cockpits.

Engine Details

Most of the 1/48-scale aircraft kits and virtually all of the 1/32-scale kits include a detailed engine. These engines, however, are only plastic moldings of the major pieces of the powerplants; the modeler must provide the intricate details like ignition lines, fuel hoses and oil lines. A photograph of the real aircraft's engine (or of a similar powerplant) is essential to give you an idea of where all these lines are routed.

The lines can be made from .002, .005, .010 and .020 inch diameter copper wire that is available from any electronics supply store. Drill holes in the engine castings with a pin vise to match the diameter of the wire. Hold the wires in the holes with a drop of cyanoacrylate cement. Small bits of decal can be used to simulate some of the warning placards and other labels on the engine.

Landing Gear Details

There is a jungle of hydraulic lines and cables grouped around and inside the landing gear bay of any aircraft that has retractable landing gear. Again, photographs of full-size aircraft landing gear are your best guide to the locations of these lines. At the very least, a length of copper wire (painted black) should be extended from the landing gear bay to the backside of the wheel to represent the hydraulic brake line. It's surprising how a single line like this can suggest that there is a whole lot more plumbing just out of sight on the other side of the landing gear strut or inside the landing gear bay. Use the same type of copper wire for these lines as for the engine detailing.

The tires on an aircraft that is resting on the ground or pavement are deformed by the weight of the aircraft. You can simulate that flat bottom and sidewall bulge by carefully heating the bottom of the tire *near* a hot woodburning pencil or soldering iron—don't touch the plastic to the hot iron or the plastic will run. When the plastic is hot, press it firmly on a block of wood to flatten the bottom of the tire. The plastic that is displaced by this will form a realistic bulge on the sidewalls. If you're worried about damaging the tires by heating them, simply file a flat spot on the bottom of each tire to simulate its contact patch.

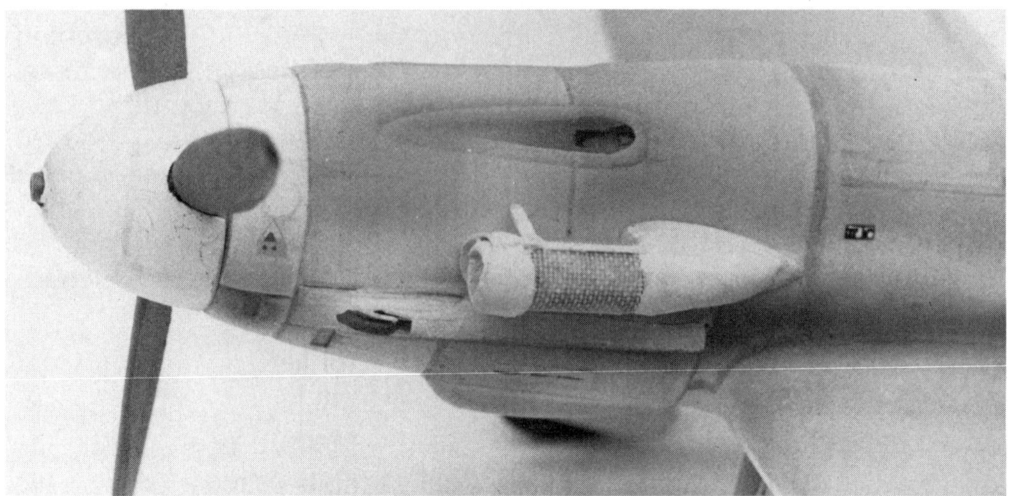

Figure 7-15. Some engine details are visible on the outside of the cowl like this desert air filter on an Me109. The screen is fine-mesh brass plumbers' screen.

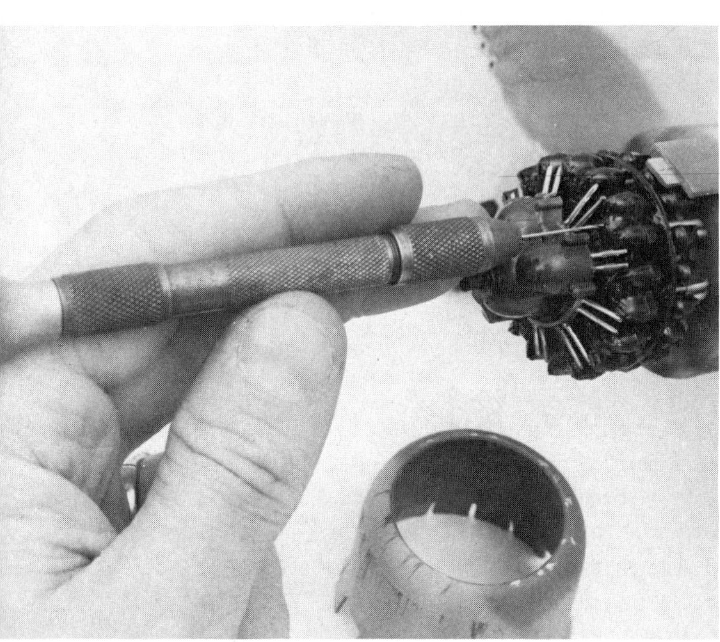

Figure 7-16. Use a pin vise to drill the engine so it will accept fine copper wires to simulate ignition wires, oil lines and fuel hoses.

Figure 7-17. Hold the plastic tire close to a woodburning pencil so the heat softens the plastic. Press the tire down on a wood surface to mold a bulging contact patch on the bottom.

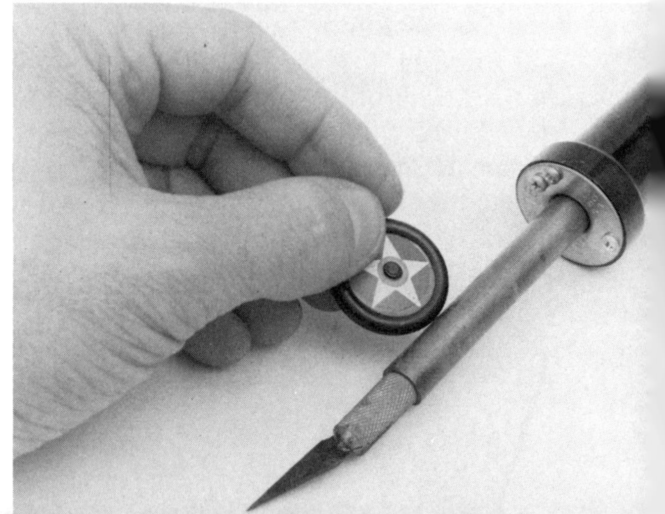

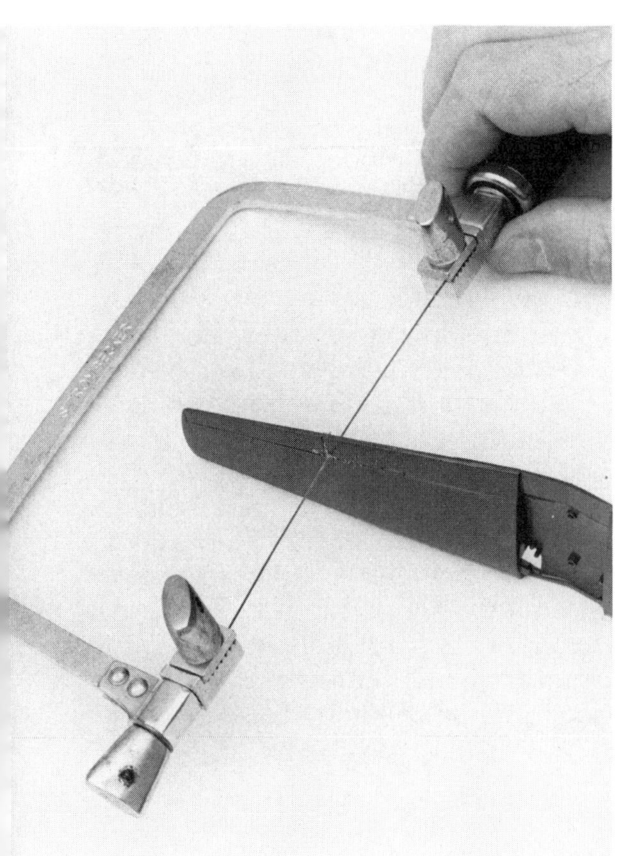

Figure 7-18. Cut any of the flaps that you want to appear in operating positions with a jeweler's saw.

Figure 7-19. The wing flaps on this 1/48-scale Me109 were vacuum-formed from .010 inch thick styrene sheet using the originals as molds. The canopy was also vacuum-formed to reduce its thickness.

Working Flaps

The control surfaces or flaps on most plastic model kits are molded in one piece with the wings, stabilizer or rudder. You can improve the realism of a model that is supposed to be resting on the ground by cutting the flaps with a jeweler's saw and cementing them back in place at a slight downward angle as they so often appear when a full-size aircraft is at rest. A jeweler's saw is a type of jigsaw that accepts a very fine-tooth blade that is also much thinner than a conventional jigsaw blade. Most hobby shops can supply jeweler's saws. Buy about a half-dozen spare blades because you will break some until you learn how fragile they can be.

Use the jeweler's saw to cut along the molded-in seams or lines that indicate where the control surfaces (flaps) are hinged. You may have to saw right across some of the tiny tabs that represent the tabs of the hinges. You can file away the tab to leave a notch and cut a fake tab from a scrap of plastic to replace the one you took from the control surface. Don't just guess how the flaps should be angled when you glue them in place; find a photo of the full-size aircraft (or a similar aircraft) at rest and install the control surfaces on your model to match. Some control surfaces are only operated with the aircraft in flight.

Chapter 8

Conversions

THE ultimate challenge that any miniatures hobby offers lies in creating something you cannot buy as a kit. One of the most rewarding achievements for an aircraft modeler is the creation of a model that is as different from that on the box lid as possible. Hobbyists often try to find a full-size aircraft that is almost the same as the one in the kit but with some outstanding feature that is different.

The conversion of a single-seat aircraft into a two-seat trainer (or vice versa) is one of the most popular conversions. A number of full-size aircraft were modified slightly during their production; the updating of a kit from its prototype to the model that succeeded that prototype is another very popular type of conversion. For example, the alteration of a Lockheed P-38L fighter to the night-fighting P-38M requires only the addition of a dome in the canopy for an observer behind the pilot and some minor detail parts. If the conversion is a relatively minor alteration to the shape of the aircraft, some kits will include the parts for both versions. In some cases you can make an "instant" conversion by applying a different paint and decal scheme to the stock kit. There are also dozens of "conversion kits" that contain only the vacuum-formed parts to alter a complete aircraft kit along with instructions for installing the parts and suggested accurate paint and markings.

Decal Conversions

Most modelers think of a conversion as the alteration of the actual shape of the model to match another version of the full-size aircraft. If you are an expert on full-size aircraft, these conversions will be a source of endless enjoyment to you. If you're a novice in this field, however, you may prefer a simpler method of converting your aircraft into a different model. There are many striking alterations that can be made to a stock kit by simply painting it a different color from that on the box art and applying a different set of decals. The firms that manufacture accessory decals for display model aircraft generally include accurate instructions for

Figure 8-1. Charles Quigley used Micro Scale's decals and painting tips to make this authentic bright red 1/48-scale P-38J "Lightning" from a Monogram kit.

painting the model as well as diagrams or profile views that show where the decals are supposed to fit. To be certain the model you build is true to life, you really should try to locate a photograph of that particular full-size aircraft in a book or magazine. The decal set and instructions alone should be enough to allow you to build a very accurate replica like the "Yippee" version of the P-38.

Figure 8-2. There really was a bright red P-38J "Lightning." Official Air Force photos are one way of assuring that your model is accurate. *Photo courtesy U.S. Air Force.*

Figure 8-3. The cockpit details and slightly worn paint are visible in this photo of "Yippee" with its near propellor stopped for the photographer. *Photo courtesy U.S. Air Force.*

Simple Conversions

You may want to make a conversion that involves subtle visual changes that are a little more complex than just a change in decals. This can still be an easy task. It's not difficult at all to fill in seams and scribe new ones or to file down the shapes of wings, rudders or stabilizers as in the following conversion.

Figure 8-4. The Revell P-39 "Airacobra" duplicates the aircraft's appearance at the start of World War II.

Figure 8-5. Walker Burton made all of the detail changes to convert the Revell 1/72-scale "Airacobra" to the tail-dragging "Airabonita."

Figure 8-6. Some conversions involve only minor detail changes, like installing flaps to hide the exhaust flames on this "night fighter" version of the Hawker "Hurricane," painted black.

The Bell Airacobra achieved fame from the fact that its engine was mounted *behind* the pilot rather than in front as it was on almost *every* other single-engine aircraft of the time. One of the variations on this theme was Bell's Airabonita. There are several Airacobra kits, and the conversion to an Airabonita is simple enough. The Airabonita's most noticeable variation was that it landed as a "tail dragger" while the Airacobra had a tricycle landing gear with a nose wheel. The wing wheels on the Airabonita, then, must be moved toward the front edges of the wings. The Airabonita also had a smaller air scoop behind the cockpit, and a pair of air scoops on the bottoms of the wings. There were minor differences in the shapes of the rudder, stabilizer, and landing gear doors. Some scraps of plastic, filler putty and a hobby knife are all that are needed to convert the Airacobra to the Airabonita.

Conversion Kits

When a conversion involves parts that are larger than those in the stock kit, the modeler can find himself with the problems of a major work of sculpture. This is where a conversion kit can help. Conversion kits contain parts and instructions that can turn a standard kit into a unique model.

The conversion of the Boeing 727 into the "stretched" Boeing 727-200 commercial aircraft could be accomplished by cutting the 727-200's extra length of fuselage from a second 727 kit. Instead, you could buy the Griffin brand conversion kit, which includes a new fuselage, vacuum-molded from sheet styrene, and instructions for using the fuselage with parts from the Airfix 1/144-scale 727 to make a near-perfect replica of the Boeing 727-200. The windows can either be drilled out of the Griffin fuselage and filed to shape or simply covered with Griffin's window decals to simulate the windows. If you do want to fit clear windows into a commercial aircraft model, you can do so (*after* the model has been assembled and painted) using common white glue for the window panes as described in Chapter 9.

The conversion kits are intended for the modeler who has developed his or her skills to at least an intermediate level of proficiency by assembling a half-dozen or more kits. The most difficult skill to acquire is the fitting and filling with putty, and that can be made more difficult with an ill-fitting injection-molded plastic kit than with any conversion or vacuum-formed kit. Less experienced modelers might be a bit frightened by the thought of cutting plastic to make a conversion, to install a conversion kit, or to assemble one of the vacuum-formed kits described in Chapter 9. When you cut your own parts, you can assure their fit while you are completing the cut. Don't worry about your ability to cut plastic with a razor saw or a jeweler's saw if you have already developed the skills of assembling out-of-the-box kits; even if you do make a mistake, you can always buy

Figure 8-7. The Griffin conversion kit for the Boeing 727-200 uses vacuum-formed parts to lengthen the Airfix 1/72-scale Boeing 727.

another kit and relegate the first one to the scrap box so the parts can be used on some later conversion.

Vacuum-Forming Techniques

The best way of shaping thin sheets of plastic to mold thinner plastic canopies, landing gear doors, cowls and panels is to pull heated plastic tightly over a form or mold with a vacuum. To vacuum-form a part you need a machine to expose the mold to a vacuum and to hold the plastic taut while it is being heated and pulled over the mold. Mattel made a toy called a Vac-U-Form in the late 1960s that was perfect for model work but these machines are now collector's items. A new firm, Idea Development, is making a wooden vacuum-forming machine called the Formicator that was designed for the folks who build flying model aircraft. The machine is large enough to mold a wing for a 1/32-scale fighter on its 6¼ x 14¾ inch vacuum surface (platten). The frame accepts 8½ x 17 inch plastic sheets but the edges of the plastic must be clamped in the frame supplied with the machine.

The Formicator operates much like the larger machines that are used to mold the vacuum-formed kits shown in Chapter 9. Since the Formicator is designed for use at home, you must supply the heat source (your home oven) and the vacuum supply (a home vacuum cleaner). The Formicator kit includes the wood parts, metal vacuum platten or base, assembly screws, a supply of plastic sheets and complete instructions. The assembled Formicator is a two-part tool: the upper portion or frame is removable, and that has its own removable frame (held in place with wing nuts) so you can clamp the plastic sheets in place. The two-piece frame and the plastic sheet are then heated in a warm (250°F) oven with the oven door open until the plastic sheet is warm enough so it sags or droops about an inch. The frame is then placed over the second part of the Formicator: the vacuum chamber. Figure 8-8 illustrates the frame in place over the vacuum chamber with a small aircraft canopy on the chamber as the mold. A sheet of .010 inch thick clear plastic is clamped into the frame and about two-thirds of the vacuum chamber is blocked off with a sheet of aluminum so more of the vacuum is directed toward the canopy mold that is to be duplicated. The vacuum hose from any portable household vacuum cleaner is then connected to the Formicator's vacuum chamber. You won't harm the vacuum cleaner in any way. The vacuum pulls the heat-softened plastic sheet tightly over the platten and the mold (the canopy, in this case) that is placed on the platten. When you have developed some experience using a vacuum-molding machine like this, you'll find you can capture details as small as a human hair on the exterior surface of the plastic.

The mold for the vacuum-formed parts can include the original canopy, cowl, or landing gear flap from the kit. If the part is hollow, like the

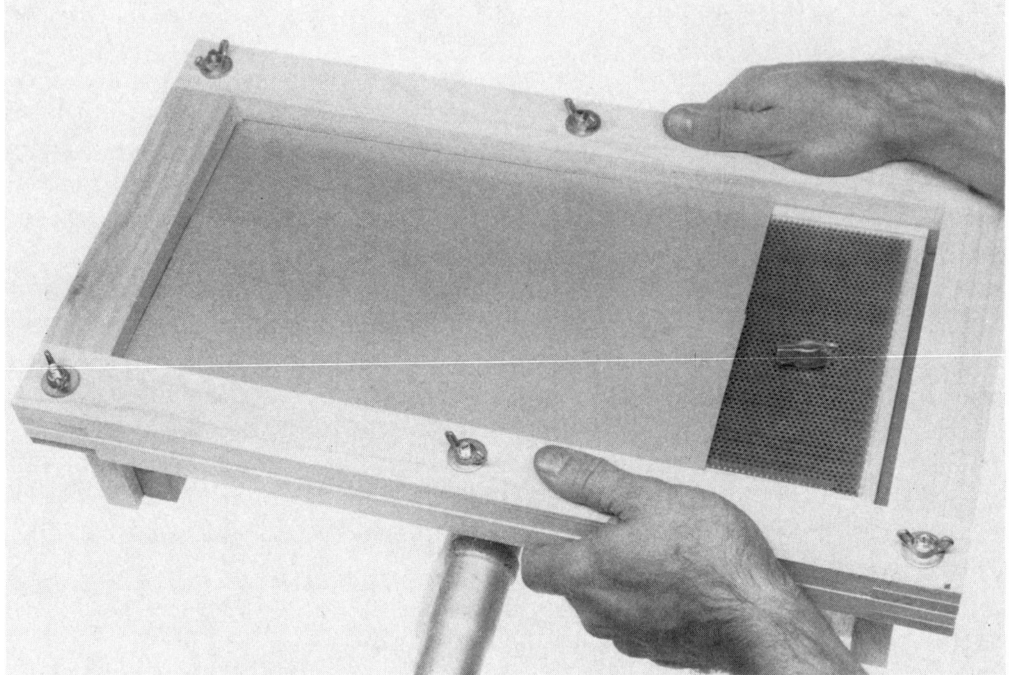

Figure 8-8. The Formicator vacuum-molding machine with a 1/72-scale canopy on the platten (right) and a household vacuum cleaner hose in place (bottom).

canopy or a cowl, you must support it with a rigid material like *water-based clay*. Be sure the clay has had at least a week to dry before touching it with the heated plastic or it could explode! Pack the inside of the part with the clay and add enough to raise the part about 1/16 inch off the vacuum chamber's platten or base. You cannot pull the plastic very far *under* the mold or pattern; the plastic will only pull *over* the part. Thus, if you have a round part that is more than half a sphere, the part must be cut in half and the vacuum-formed duplicates made in two pieces that are glued together when the model is assembled. You can mold some of the 1930-era engine cowls in one piece by placing the clay-reinforced cowl on the platten as though it were an upside-down cup.

There are several pages of instructions included with the Formicator that will give you the benefit of others' experience. I would also recommend that you assemble at least one of the vacuum-formed aircraft kits in Chapter 9 to become familiar with just what can be done with vacuum-forming and how to work with the parts that are made with the process.

The International Plastic Modelers Society

When you are ready to consider conversions, you're ready to join the organization of modelers that caters to those whose hobby is the assembly, detailing or modification of plastic miniatures. The International

Figure 8-9. This early "Warhawk" conversion is a combination of the usual P-40E parts with the P-36 to make the P-40C version of the aircraft.

Figure 8-10. The long pod beneath the center of the fuselage was the only change needed to make the gliderbomb-carrier conversion of this Hasegawa 1/32-scale Fw190A.

Plastic Modelers Society publishes a quarterly magazine that includes several ideas for conversions. Monthly newsletters as well as the bulletins from local chapters of the society have more information about kit painting and conversions. The IPMS holds a national convention and contest in America each year and the individual chapters have at least one contest each year. There is probably an IPMS chapter within 20 miles of your home if you live in a major city; if not, you may be able to start your own chapter through some of your local hobby shops. Contact the IPMS for the current annual membership fee which includes a subscription to their bimonthly *Update* and the quarterly *Review*. Membership will also provide the addresses of the various IPMS chapters. Write to IPMS/U.S.A. at P.O. Box 2555, Long Beach, CA 90801. You can receive a sample of *Update* from them for $2.00.

The IPMS publications are just one source of how-to-do-it aircraft conversion articles; similar articles are regular features in the British publication *Scale Models* and in the American publication *Scale Modeler*. I would strongly suggest that you gather your conversion information from existing conversion kits or from articles in the magazines. It's frustrating to spend weeks on a conversion only to find out that it is, was, or soon will be available as a kit. The twin fuselage version of the popular P-51D Mustang the F-82, was once a popular conversion until Monogram introduced their 1/72-scale kit.

Let the experienced modelers do the research to determine if a kit is available or planned and let them find the basic data on the full-size aircraft. You can generally build several variations of any of the conversion kits or the aircraft in the published articles by simply painting the aircraft and applying decals to match another squadron or the camouflage scheme of a similar prototype.

Chapter 9

Vacuum-Formed Models

PLASTIC model kits are made by one of two different manufacturing processes. The plastic can be melted into a fluid and injected into cavities in steel molds to make the familiar injection-molded kits sold by firms like Revell and Airfix. The second process is a bit simpler; a plastic sheet is heated and then pulled over or into the mold by vacuum. The vacuum-molded plastic molds or dies are only about 1/100 as expensive to make as those for an injection-molded model kit, but the manufacturing process for vacuum-molded kits takes about 200 times as long as the injection-molding process. The net result is that the vacuum-molded kits are often twice as expensive as a similar injection-molded kit.

The modeler is the one who benefits from the existence of the vacuum-molded kits because the process allows a manufacturer to offer models that would not be popular enough to sell as injection-molded kits. Almost any injection-molded kit must sell about a million kits for the manufacturer to make a profit—the vacuum-formed kits seldom sell more than a few thousand. If you're a real enthusiast, the vacuum-formed kits provide extremely well-detailed replicas of some pretty obscure aircraft. There are now just about as many different vacuum-formed kits, from almost as many manufacturers, as there are injection-molded kits.

Sheet Plastic Detail

Earlier vacuum-formed kits lacked much of the surface detail that was standard on injection-molded models. These early kits were made by pulling the sheet plastic *over* the mold, which served as a "male" pattern. The detail was on the inside of the plastic rather than on the outside where it belonged. Today, most of the vacuum-molded kits are made with "female" molds where the plastic is pulled *into* a cavity so the detail is on the outside of the part. The better kits capture as many rivet and panel details as the best injection-molded kits. The kits now include injection-molded detail parts like engines, landing gear, propellors and other parts that are almost impossible to mold from sheets of plastic.

The one area where a vacuum-formed kit cannot match an injection-molded kit is in ease of assembly. The modeler must carefully trim the vacuum-formed parts from the scrap sheet of plastic as shown in this

Figure 9-1. The vacuum-formed kits offer miniatures of some unusual aircraft like this J&L kit for the Stinson Model 'T' Tri-Motor.

chapter. This is not a difficult task but it does take a bit more time and effort than just clipping injection-molded parts from their molding sprues. The list of manufacturers of vacuum-formed kits increases every year. Some of the current manufacturers are Aeroform, Airframe, Airtec, Combat, Dragon, Griffin, J & L, Nova, Rareplanes, and Sutcliff.

Assembling Vacuum-Formed Models

The selection of new vacuum-formed miniature aircraft kits is growing much faster than the selection of new injection-molded kits. The kit manufacturers who use the injection-molding process just cannot afford to cut more than one or two new dies each year; besides, there are already several thousand injection-molding dies that are still in perfect condition. The result is that the manufacturers of injection-molded kits "cycle" their kits so that only about one-fourth to one-half of their total line is on the market in any given year. Usually, when the older kits are reintroduced, they have new packing with new decals and new color schemes on the

Figure 9-2. The metal-filled epoxy molds that J&L Aircraft Models uses to female-mold the Stinson Model 'T' Tri-Motor.

Figure 9-3. Cut-away views showing female-molded (left) and male-molded (right) vacuum-formed parts. The figure also shows where to score (cut) the parts to snap them from the sheet, and where to sand them to shape.

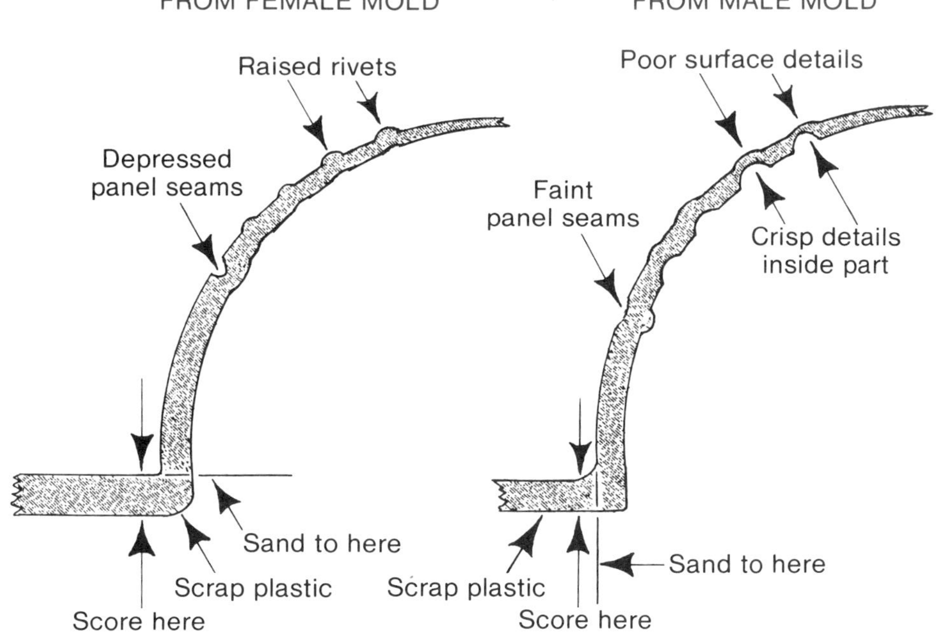

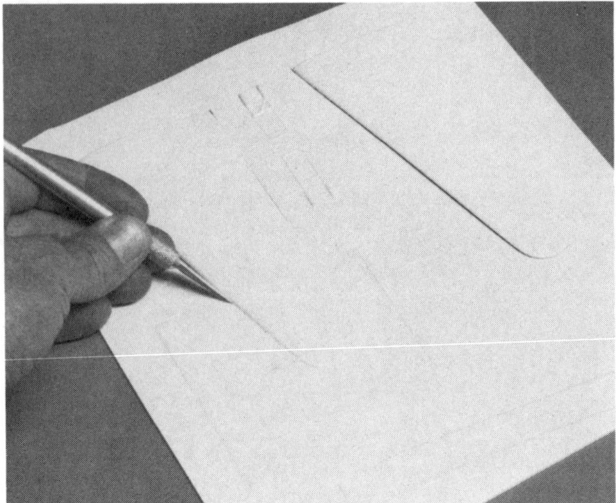

Figure 9-4. Cut vertically along the edges of the parts of a kit made with female molds.

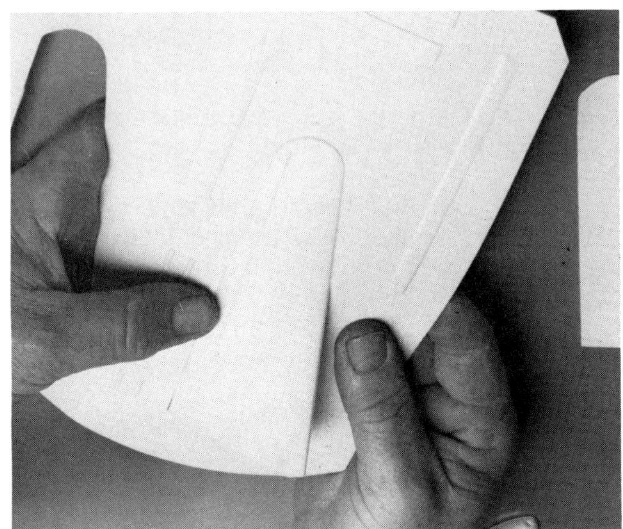

Figure 9-5. Gently bend the scrap plastic back and forth along the cut lines to break the parts from the sheet plastic.

box to match. You probably won't be able to resist the appeal of the miniature aircraft kits that are made with the vacuum-forming process so you might as well learn how to build them.

Figure 9-3 illustrates a cut-away view through one-fourth of a typical aircraft fuselage that has been molded in vacuum-formed plastic. If you examine the parts in a kit, you can determine whether the kit was made with the female-molding process or the male-molding process. The details on the male-molded parts will be so vague that it will be extremely difficult to finish one of these kits to the standards of your injection-molded models. It is possible, of course, to scribe new panel lines and even to make new rivets but the process requires a considerable amount of time and patience.

Figure 9-6. Hold each part with a loop of masking tape while you move it back and forth on fine-grit sandpaper.

Figure 9-7. The final sanding should be done on number 400 wet-or-dry sandpaper wetted with water.

Talk to your hobby dealer about the kit, if he would rather not open the sealed package, and try to determine which of the brands he carries has the best detail and is easiest to assemble. The first vacuum-formed kit you build should be a relatively simple model, like a single-engine fighter or private plane, so you can get the feel of working with this type of kit.

The key to assembling a vacuum-formed model lies in cutting the parts from their molding sheets. The cross-sectional views show how the plastic is formed at the right-angle corners where the part ends and the flat scrap plastic sheet begins. Most of the vacuum-formed kit manufacturers try to mold in a line near this corner to show you precisely where the part ends and the scrap begins. Do *not* try to cut the part on that line—*do* try to cut the part from the scrap plastic sheet so there is about 1/64 inch of scrap beside that "cut" line so you can file and sand the part to exact size. Some of the early vacuum-formed kits did not make allowances for the plastic that is "lost" in that right-angle bend between part and scrap. Examine the parts in your kit carefully to see if that might be the case and, if it is, you must sand and file the *vertical* edge or surface as shown for the female-molded part in figure 9-3.

Cutting Out the Parts   Do not try to cut all the way through the plastic with a hobby knife. All of the vacuum-formed kits use some type of styrene plastic which, if scored lightly, will break when you bend it. Use a very sharp hobby knife to make a light cut all around the edge of the part. Refer to figure 9-3 to determine how far from the part the initial cut should be—*always* leave at least 1/64 inch of scrap on the part so you can file the scrap away to get a perfect fit. Slice lightly all around the part, overlapping each cut when you have to lift the knife, so there is no area left without at least a light cut. Break the part from the flat plastic sheet by bending it back and forth along the lightly cut lines. Hold your fingers as close to the cuts as you can while you wiggle the part up and down. Use this method to remove all of the parts from the flat plastic sheet.

The ragged edges of the parts will disappear when you sand the joining surfaces. Glue a piece of fine-grit sandpaper or emery paper to a perfectly flat block of wood, and glue a piece of number 400 wet-or-dry sandpaper or emery paper to a second flat block of wood. Rub the vacuum-formed kit parts against the fine-grit sandpaper using a loop of masking tape as a handle. The masking tape can be used to lift one edge of the part a bit, as you sand, if that is needed to obtain a perfectly flat surface. Check the joining surface of the part frequently so you don't remove too much of the plastic. When the joint is within a hair's width of being right, finish the surface by rubbing the part against the number 400 wet-or-dry sandpaper block. Wet the sandpaper with water occasionally so the sandpaper will remain cool and will not melt the soft plastic. Test-fit each part as you sand it. You may need to wrap some fine-grit and some number 400-grit sandpaper around a short piece of broom handle or a paintbrush handle to make a round sanding block for shaping concave areas like wing joints.

Applying Cement   The styrene plastic used for most vacuum-formed kits is softer than the plastic used for most injection-molded kits and it is often a bit thinner. If you use tube-type cement for plastics, the solvents in the cement will remain volatile long enough to melt and sag the thinner styrene plastic joints. *Use only liquid cement* for plastics on any vacuum-formed kit. Apply the cement with a number 00 paintbrush or a draftsman's ruling pen so you can control each and every drop. Paint a very thin layer of the cement on the joining faces of one half of a wing or fuselage and immediately press the other half against it. Apply more cement to the joint, a single drop at a time. Watch the cement flow along

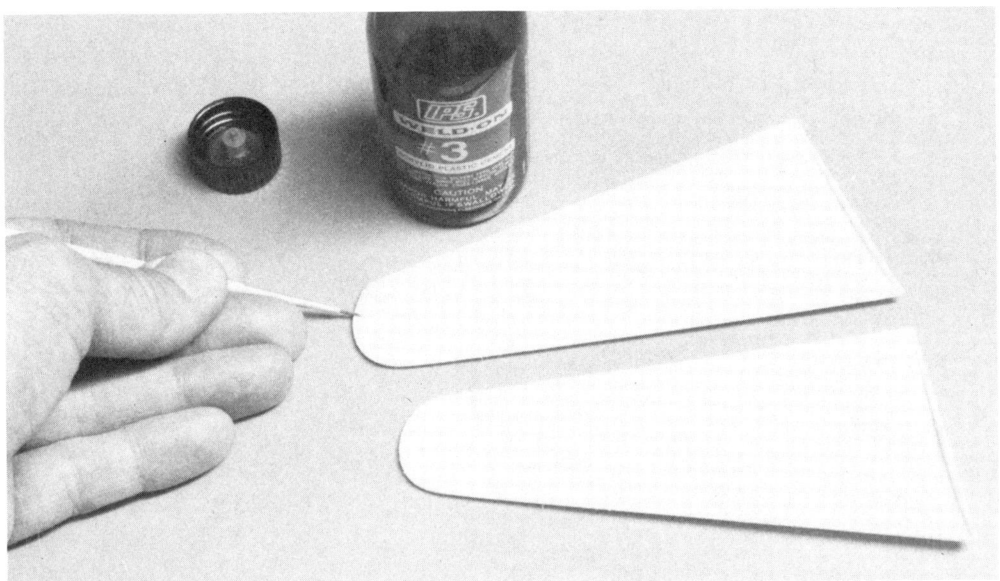

Figure 9-8. Apply liquid cement around the inner edges of one half of the wing, then press the halves together immediately and apply a bit more cement.

the seam by capillary action so you will apply just enough cement to completely cover the joint. If you use too much liquid cement it, too, can melt and distort the joint.

The thin joining surfaces of the fuselage can often be assembled more easily and precisely if you cut some strips of the leftover flat styrene sheet that are 1/8 inch wide by 1 or 2 inches long for use as reinforcing and alignment tabs. Glue the tabs inside the first half of the fuselage but test-fit the second half as you go to be sure the tabs really do help to align the two fuselage halves. Cut small aligning tabs from the flat styrene sheet if you have trouble aligning or fitting a wing or engine. The vacuum-formed kits cannot include the alignment pins, tabs and interlocks of the injected-molded kits so you may have to make a few of your own. Some kits also need extra bulkheads or reinforcing ribs for the wings. If those parts are needed, they are generally described in the kit's instructions.

Allow lots of time for the cement to dry on the vacuum-formed models. It is generally wise to leave the model in a well-ventilated area for about a week. The body filler putty that is used on injection-molded model seams works just as well with the vacuum-formed kits. The solvents in the putty can melt the plastic, so apply only 1/32-inch thick layers of putty to any seam or depression. Give the putty about 72 hours to dry completely before sanding it with wet number 600 wet-or-dry sandpaper for a smooth and even edge. Misalignment can occur at the seams of a vacuum-formed model so take some extra time to inspect it and, if necessary, apply several layers of filler putty until the seams are perfect. Any rivet or panel lines that have disappeared during the filling and sanding

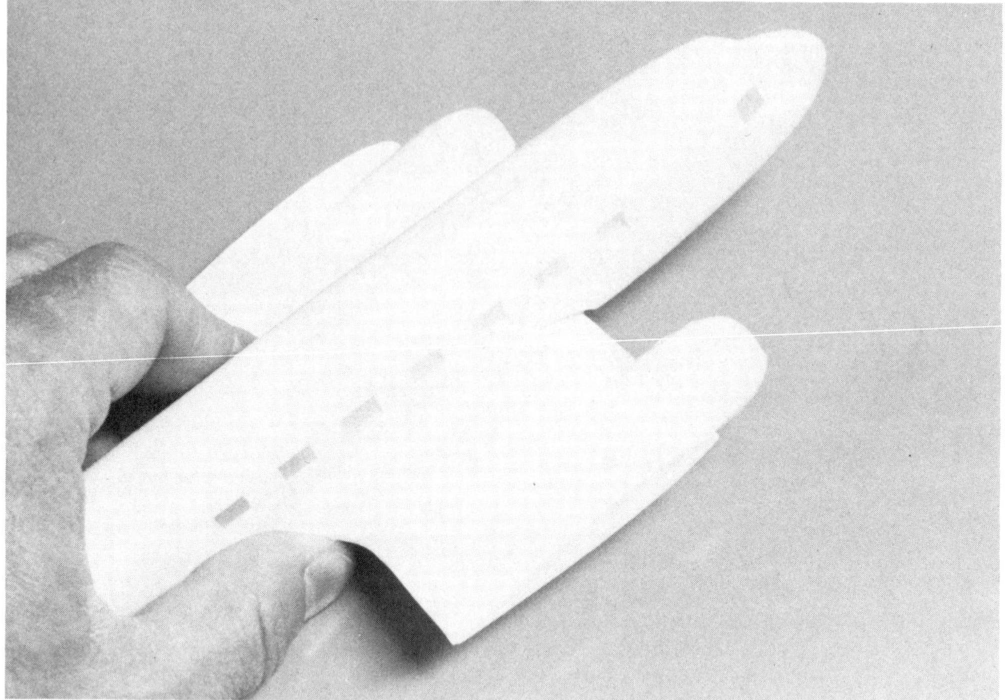

Figure 9-9. When the seams are filled and the model is painted, the vacuum-formed kits can be extremely realistic.

can be replaced using the techniques shown in Chapter 7. The model can now be painted and marked with decals using the same techniques as for injection-molded kits.

Installing Windows

The multitude of small windows in a commercial aircraft can be installed in the fuselage of a vacuum-formed model using one of two methods. The easiest way to install small windows in any model kit should be done after the model is completely assembled, painted and decaled. Simply spread a drop of white glue around the edges of the window opening with a toothpick. When the toothpick is removed slowly, the glue will remain behind as a bubble that will dry almost clear and flush with the surface of the model. The only disadvantage is that the windows will be slightly cloudy.

If you want truly clear windows, you'll need to cut each one from clear plastic. Most kits include clear styrene plastic which can be glued with model cement. You can also purchase sheets of .010 inch thick Evergreen brand clear styrene at most model railroad shops. It is possible to install clear windows after the fuselage is assembled but the task is much easier if you complete it while the fuselage is still in two halves.

Figure 9-10. The vacuum-formed kits sometimes have several subassemblies, like this J&L 1/72-scale DC-2 kit, for extra strength.

Figure 9-11. Jack Stackhouse finished this J&L 1/72-scale Douglas DC-2 with the kit's TWA decals.

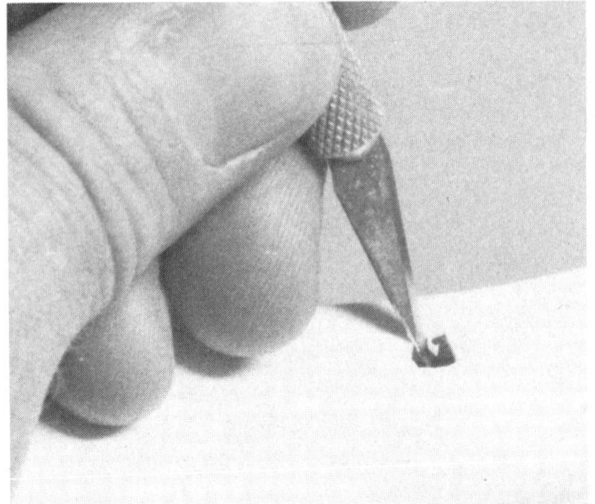

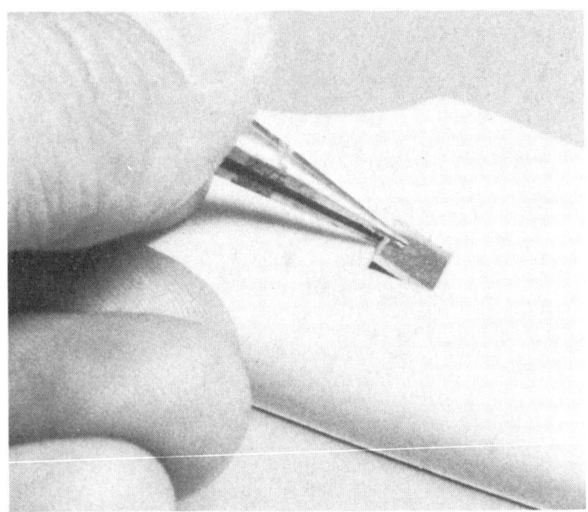

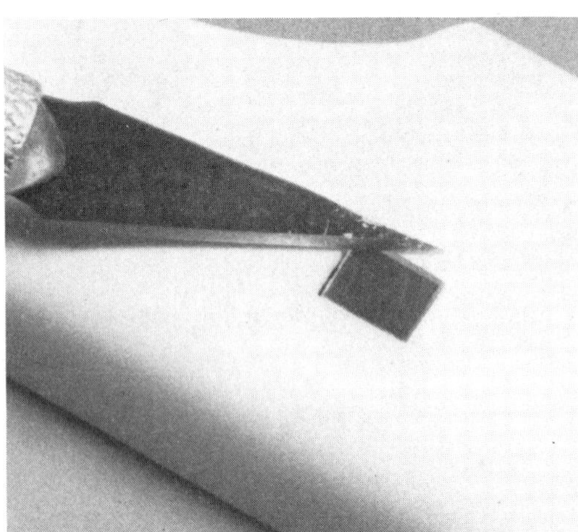

Figure 9-12. Gouge out the center of each window with the tip of a sharp hobby knife before the fuselage halves are assembled.

Figure 9-13. Cut clear styrene plastic sheet to fit the window opening and lay it in place. No other type of clear plastic will work, here.

Figure 9-14. Use a hobby knife to press the plastic window firmly into its opening so that about .005 inch of the plastic protrudes from the surface.

Figure 9-15. Polish the styrene windows to remove all traces of sanding scratches.

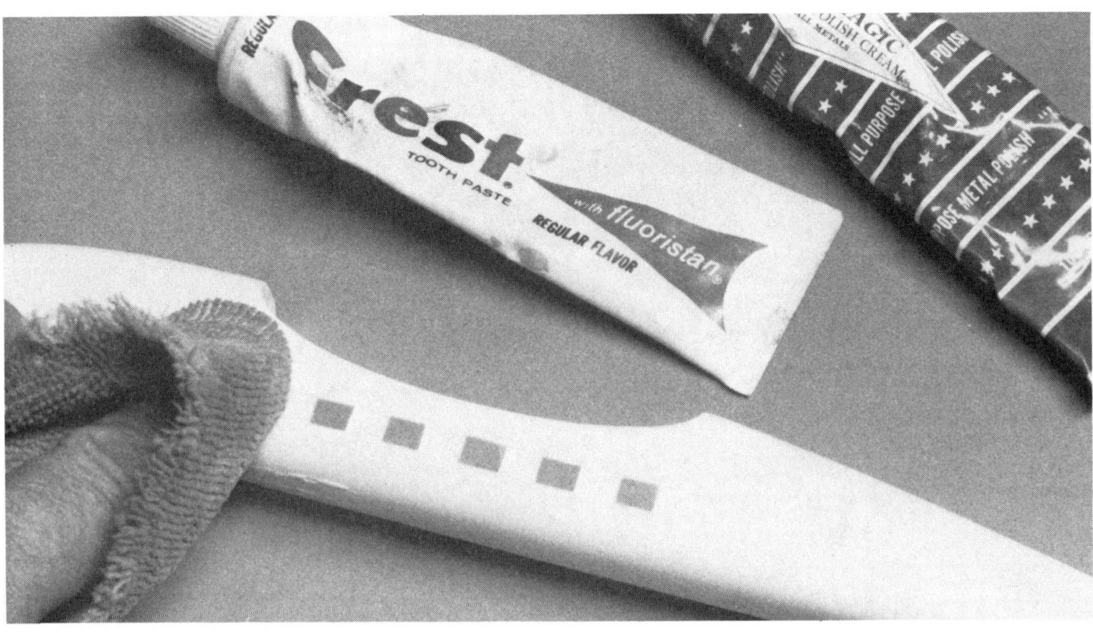

Figure 9-16. The cut-and-fit method can also be used to make the clear windowpanes on aircraft cockpits.

Cut the windows out of the fuselage gouging the center of each window with a sharp hobby knife. Then work the knife around until you have a hole large enough for the knife to fit through to shave the edges of the window to size. Cut the clear styrene plastic to fit the openings by tracing the size of the opening directly onto the clear plastic with a hobby knife. Cement the windows in place with a single drop of liquid cement for plastics and allow the cement to dry for about 48 hours. The windows should protrude from the fuselage about the thickness of a sheet of paper.

When the glue has dried, sand the windows flush with the surface of the fuselage with number 400 wet-or-dry sandpaper dipped frequently into water. The glue marks and scratches from the sandpaper can be removed by polishing the windows with fine aluminum polish like Blue Magic or with toothpaste. Mask each of the windows with clear masking fluid when you paint the aircraft.

Vacuum-formed kits that require canopies generally include a vacuum-formed clear plastic canopy. Vacuum-formed canopies are usually much thinner and more realistic than injection-molded canopies. The canopy must be lightly cut and the excess plastic broken away as with a plastic wing or fuselage part. Sand the canopy so it fits the fuselage precisely.

Chapter 10

Historical Miniatures

THERE are almost as many reasons why folks enjoy the hobby of building model aircraft as there are folks. The hobby offers considerably more scope than you might guess from examining the bits of plastic inside a kit box. Some miniature aircraft enthusiasts enjoy building kits more than they do painting them, others search out the most obscure prototypes for models to convert, while others spend a good part of their leisure time reading books and magazines to collect research data for their models. Doing research to build unusual and historically accurate miniature aircraft is almost a hobby within the hobby. Dozens of magazines and thousands of books have been published illustrating and describing full-size aircraft from every era.

There are so many kits on the market that you can build an incredibly complete collection of aircraft from any time period including the World War I era right up to the present and beyond to projected aircraft of the future. Yet you don't have to turn a page in any book or magazine to build historically-accurate models; the aircraft that is illustrated on the kit box lid is probably a good example of how the model in the kit looked during at least one point in its history. You just may find the hobby to be more enjoyable than you ever imagined, however, if you try to find other examples of the aircraft to duplicate using the same kit but different paint and decals.

Decal Sets

Any aircraft modeler could build as many as a thousand historically accurate replicas of real aircraft without ever opening another book or magazine. The simple shortcut is to select kits that are readily available at both toy and hobby stores and paint them to match the instructions included with accessory decal sets. The decal makers, like Micro Scale and Scale-Master, spend countless hours searching through books and magazines and government documents to find unusual and attractive markings for most of the plastic aircraft kits on the market. The majority of the thousands of decal sets are intended for the most popular kits. There are also decal sets that offer several variations of markings for limited production vacuum-formed aircraft and conversion kits.

Figure 10-1. There is an incredible number of photos of World War II aircraft, like this Lockheed P-38J "Lightning," available in thousands of books. *U.S. Air Force photo.*

Figure 10-2. Four P-38J "Lightnings" in very tight formation. *U.S. Air Force photo.*

If you don't want to try matching the accessory decals to kits, just choose one of the more popular injection-molded plastic miniatures and you should have no trouble locating decals to fit them. Your local hobby shop can be a great help because you can buy both the kit and the decals at the same time. Many of the decal sets include markings for several different aircraft. If you find that two or more of these markings appeal to you, buy the additional kits right on the spot. Aircraft kits, even from the major manufacturers, are often dropped from production for indefinite periods of time, so it's best to buy a kit you want when you see it and then store it away.

Most of the decal sets include a drawing that indicates where the decals are to be applied with notes on the appropriate colors for the aircraft. Thus, you can build a reasonably accurate replica of the full-size aircraft using nothing more than the basic plastic kit, the accessory decals and paint. Be sure to save any decals from the kit or from the accessory

Figure 10-3. Charles Quigley used the instructions from Micro Scale's decal set to paint and decal his 1/72-scale Airfix P-38F.

Figure 10-4. Some of the Revell 1/32-scale P-38J kits include extra parts to duplicate the "droop snoot" radar version of the aircraft.

decal packs that are leftover when you finish the model. A scrapbox of decals can be extremely helpful when you ruin a decal or when a special decal is needed for a variation of some other kit.

Documentation

Most modelers find the hobby most satisfying when they build replicas of aircraft they have located in books or magazines. There's a greater thrill from creating a replica of any aircraft if you've found photographs of the full-size aircraft to supplement the kit instructions and decals. The instructions furnished with many decal sets include references to books and magazines that have photos of the full-size aircraft. The photographs are

Figure 10-5. Official Air Force photographs in books and magazines were used by Charles Quigley to detail the interior of his 1/48-scale Monogram P-38J.

Figure 10-6. Published photos of full-size aircraft often include detailing shots like this that displays the engine bays of the P-38J. *U.S. Air Force photo.*

indispensable for adding details like special guns, drop tanks, landing gear, and radio antennae that may have appeared only on the particular aircraft you want to build.

If you intend to enter your model in any of the local or national International Plastic Modelers Society contests, research is a must. Unlike those for *flying* miniature aircraft, the IPMS contests usually don't require photos and a complete bibliography of the full-size aircraft—but you may be judged by a modeler who knows the prototype for your kit better than the kit manufacturer. Some of the IPMS members are pilots who may have actually flown the aircraft you are modeling.

The rewards for researching the full-size aircraft will be mostly a matter of personal pride. You will know beyond any doubt that your miniature is a precise historical replica of one particular full-size aircraft exactly as it appeared at one particular moment in its active career.

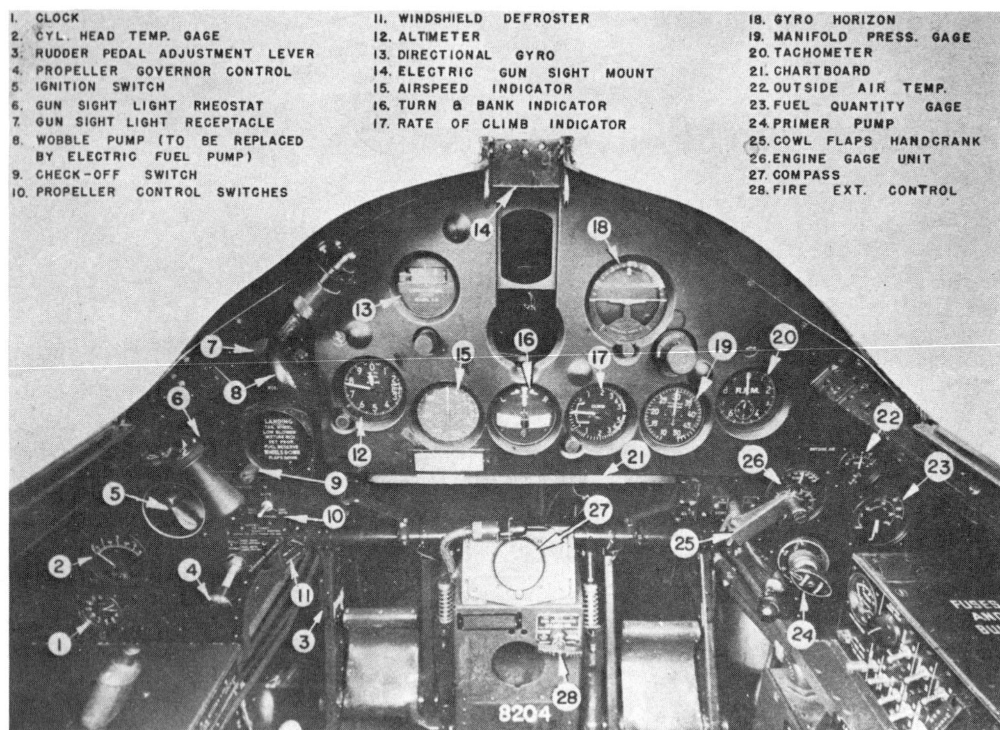

Figure 10-7. Use photos to give each aircraft its own distinctive instrument panel. This shows the interior of the FM2 "Wildcat." *U.S. Air Force photo.*

Period Pieces

You may want to concentrate your modeling skills on the period of aircraft history that appeals to you more than any other. Modelers who specialize in aircraft from just one period can develop special skills in assembling and painting their models that make the hobby more enjoyable. If you are modeling mostly World War II-era aircraft, you may want to become proficient in the use of the weathering and aging techniques in Chapter 6. If you prefer to specialize in replicas of modern commercial aircraft, you'll want to hone your skills in applying decal stripes using the techniques from Chapter 5. Modelers who build collections of World War I era-aircraft become expert in adding extra details to exposed engines and in duplicating the rigging wires and cables that braced the cloth-covered wings and stabilizers.

If you do specialize in just one period of aircraft history, you'll undoubtedly want to include some conversions, some vacuum-formed kits and perhaps even some of your own creations in your collection. You may, for example, want to duplicate all of the aircraft that participated in a particular battle or in a remote theatre of operation during World War II. Most of the aircraft will certainly be available as kits but you may need

Figure 10-8. The early years of aircraft history are covered by a variety of kits, including this trio of 1908–1910 machines from Entex. *Photo courtesy Entex Industries.*

Figure 10-9. The trim shape and ship-like rigging of the World War I-era aircraft, like this Revell 1/72-scale Fokker D-VII, make them fascinating subjects for a collection of historical miniatures.

Figure 10-10. Some WWI aircraft were painted aluminum colors over a fabric skin.

to create rare aircraft through conversions or the use of vacuum-formed kits. Some of the most interesting and esoteric models are replicas of "enemy" aircraft that were captured and repainted by the opposing forces; American P-47 Thunderbolts in German markings are certain to attract some special attention from other modelers.

Peacetime Aircraft

The majority of models available in any scale are replicas of fighters, bombers or other warplanes. The most popular "new" category of model aircraft kits, though, includes commercial and private aircraft. The history

Figure 10-11. The Japanese Mitsubishi A6M5 "Zero" from World War II is one of the most popular aircraft miniatures. This is the Minicraft/Hasegawa 1/32-scale kit. *Photo courtesy Minicraft Models, Inc.*

Figure 10-12. The Minicraft/Hasegawa 1/72-scale model of the Japanese Mitsubishi G4M1 "Betty" bomber that carried the rare "Ohka" flying bomb. *Photo courtesy Minicraft Models, Inc.*

of aircraft as transportation is beginning to receive the attention of both the model kit manufacturers and, of course, their customers. There are almost as many new manufacturing dies being cut for models of commercial and private aircraft as there are for warplanes. Many of the "missing" prototype aircraft are being offered either as vacuum-formed conversions for existing injection-molded kits or as complete vacuum-formed kits. Part of this trend is the result of the fact that virtually every warplane, no matter how obscure, is available as a kit or a simple conversion. The decal manufacturers are following this same trend by offering a rainbow of colors for kits of past and present airliners.

If you find this area of the hobby to your liking, I would strongly recommend that you purchase any kits that appeal to you as they appear on the market; the kit manufacturers are taking maximum advantage of the variety of commercial airline markings to offer limited-production runs of airliners with decals for specific airlines. If you see a kit with airline markings that you like, buy it just to be certain you have the proper decals. The kit itself will probably be around for decades but those particular markings as well as the box lid may soon be collector's items.

Helicopters

Whirlybirds are another popular category among aircraft modelers. There certainly are not as many different kits for helicopters as there are for winged aircraft, but there are several dozen helicopter models in all the popular scales. The helicopter models often become collector's items more rapidly than most aircraft miniatures because there is a relatively limited market for them. Injection-molded and vacuum-formed kits have been produced for the majority of the full-size commercial and wartime

Figure 10-14. The vacuum-formed kit makers are producing kits for peacetime aircraft as well as warplanes. This is J&L Aircraft Models' 1/72-scale Curtiss-Wright T-32 "Condor."

Figure 10-15. Entex Industries offers this injection-molded plastic kit of the famous Hughes "Spruce Goose." Even in 1/200 scale the model has a 19-inch wingspan. *Photo courtesy Entex Industries.*

Figure 10-13. The Griffin vacuum-formed 1/144-scale Viscount 745 turboprop airliner with Scale-Master decals for the circa 1961 Capital Airlines markings. Lloyd Jones assembled and painted the kit.

helicopters over the years. However, you may not find more than a dozen different models in even the largest hobby shops.

If you want to start a collection of helicopter models, you'd be wise to purchase the models as you see them because they may be taken off the market a few months after their introduction. The situation is really no different from that of any specialized area of the plastic model aircraft hobby. There are molds in existence, somewhere, for probably about 10,000 different aircraft models, but only about a thousand of them are in production during any given year. Sometimes the old molds are revived and the collector's kits will reappear on the market but you never know when or if that will happen. That's why the real enthusiasts in our hobby have shelves full of kits, enough to last them for ten years. You may only have one chance to purchase a kit before it becomes a collector's item.

Publications

The Sources section of this book lists several magazines that include feature articles on historical aircraft. Most of the magazines deal almost exclusively with full-size aircraft but many of the articles are written *for*

Figure 10-16. This rare aircraft was built from a 1/72-scale Dragon Model Works' vacuum-formed kit for the world's first flying jet floatplane, the Saunders Roe SRA-1.

Figure 10-17. Monogram's 1/72-scale bomber series includes some really impressive models like this B-52 with a 30-inch wingspan.

Figure 10-18. A pair of 1/72-scale Revell F-4U "Phantom" fighters in U.S. Air Force and Royal Air Force markings.

(and sometimes by) modelers. Color profile views of aircraft from all eras are a regular feature of magazines like *Air International.* Other magazines feature color photos and paintings as well as scale plans to help you determine decal and marking positions more accurately.

The Sources section lists only a few of the major publishers and some of the mail order book dealers who specialize in books on full-size aircraft. There are *thousands* of books illustrating aircraft from *every* era. Many of these volumes are designed to supply just the information you need to create truly unique markings for miniature aircraft. Some of the books deal with just one particular aircraft while others describe the air forces of entire countries or document the history of individual aircraft manufacturers. You may be surprised to discover how many of these books are available at your local public library. These information sources are accurate enough to be used as bibliographies for college or high school research papers on historical subjects. Some of the books are developments of graduate thesis work by college students; others have been documented by pilots, mechanics and even the engineers that created the full-size aircraft designs.

Chapter 11

Display Cases and Dioramas

THE hobby of building display model aircraft does not end when the model is completed. In fact, that is the point where the major problems begin for some of us. A completed miniature aircraft is a source of pride for the first few weeks after it has been completed. In time, though, the model may find its way into the garbage if you don't have some place to display it. Plastic models are just not rugged enough to withstand the rigors of display on an open shelf. But models can survive in perfect condition for decades if they are protected from the harshness of the outside world. Dust and airborne dirt seldom do any permanent damage to a model aircraft, particularly if you have protected its surface with a coat of clear paint. It's the process of removing that dust and dirt that is certain to destroy almost any plastic model within a year or two.

Most of the people who will view your collection of miniature aircraft have an automatic response system that helps them to mentally block out the model's surroundings so they can imagine the model sitting on a runway or, perhaps, actually flying. But if your collection includes more than a dozen models, the jungle of wings and fuselages is just too much for anyone to ignore. You can avoid this confusion by placing your models in an appropriate setting in the form of a diorama. A diorama is nothing more than a display base for the model with the surface of the wooden base detailed to duplicate what might have surrounded the full-size aircraft at rest.

The Showcase

The best home for a miniature aircraft collection is a display case. This fact often escapes modelers who try to substitute everything imaginable for a display case. A bookcase won't do anything to protect the models, and hanging them from the ceiling on nylon lines just exposes every surface to airborne dirt and dust.

The item you need is either a commercial display cabinet like those that are used in stores or a piece of furniture for the home that is intended to display fine china or books. The display cases with glass tops and fronts used in stores are most practical for displaying models because they are designed with proper lighting systems built into the case. It is possible to

Figure 11-1. Plexiglas 1/8 inch thick can be used to build display cases for individual aircraft models.

install similar lighting systems in china cabinets or glass-front bookcases but you must be extremely careful to avoid the danger of fire from the heat of the light bulbs and from the electrical cords. I would strongly suggest that you contact a firm that builds display cases for stores to install lighting fixtures in a bookcase or china cabinet. The commercial cabinet-maker can determine if, for example, a small fan will be needed to ventilate the cabinet so the heat from the lamps does not cause a fire danger. That heat can often be enough to melt and warp your plastic models. The lighting fixtures in any display case for plastic models should be fluorescent to minimize the amount of heat in the confined display area.

There are dozens of types of display cases that can be used to cover just one model. Some hobby shops carry kits to build clear Plexiglas cases like the one in figure 11-1. You can build your own using 1/8 inch or thicker Plexiglas panels that can be precut to size at the store where you buy the plastic. There are several suppliers of commercial plastic materials in every major city and most are listed in the telephone book's Yellow Pages under the heading "Plastics—Rods, Tubes, Sheets, etc.—Supply Centers." These same firms will have the special cement needed for Plexiglas.

The plastic supply store may also stock clear plastic domes or bubbles in diameters up to 3 feet. These bubbles can be used, over round display bases, as an alternative style of display cabinet for an individual aircraft. The plastic for any display cover must be at least 1/16 inch thick or the material will be too weak to withstand frequent dusting and cleaning. The thin plastic covers for orchids and similar types of product packaging are just not suitable as display cases because the plastic is too thin.

Figure 11-2. A wood plaque from a craft supply store and an engraved corner plate add a touch of museum quality to Dennis Nowicki's 1/72-scale Hasegawa P-47D.

Figure 11-3. Dennis Nowicki used Preiser HO-scale race car mechanics and Woodland Scenics ground-foam rubber "grass" for his effective diorama.

The World of the Diorama

The purpose of a diorama is to surround the model with enough relevant background so the viewer does not have to tax his or her imagination to think of the aircraft as being real. From the modeler's point of view, the diorama can be as much fun to build as the aircraft itself.

You may not want to build a diorama for every one of your aircraft because you may want to imagine that some of them are in flight. Most modelers build their aircraft with the landing gear down. These models lend themselves nicely to a landing field display. You can certainly imagine that the aircraft is in flight with the landing gear down for an imminent landing or from a take-off. It's really not practical to try to build a diorama of an aircraft in flight—the nylon string from the ceiling trick or "clouds" of cotton look like nylon strings and cotton no matter how creative your imagination may be.

The diorama must be an appropriate match for the aircraft that is displayed on it: a naval aircraft looks best on an aircraft carrier deck, a launching platform or, if it's a seaplane, on a small bit of "ocean." World War I-era aircraft are excellent in dioramas that depict grass landing fields.

Figure 11-4. A portion of a wooden aircraft carrier deck on the back of a picture frame is used to display this super-detailed Minicraft/Hasegawa 1/32-scale "Zero" built by Kenneth King.

Figure 11-5. Plastic strips can be drilled to simulate the deck tiedown panels of the carrier with balsa strips for the decking.

Figure 11-6. Paper facial tissue makes fine scale model tarps if painted with appropriate shades of khaki and tied down with beige or yellow sewing thread to simulate hemp rope.

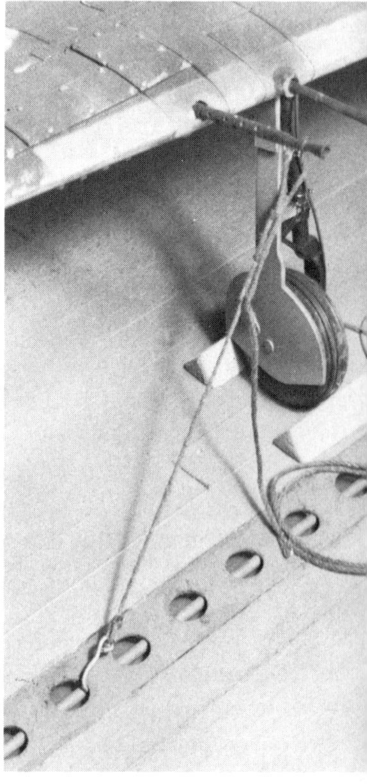

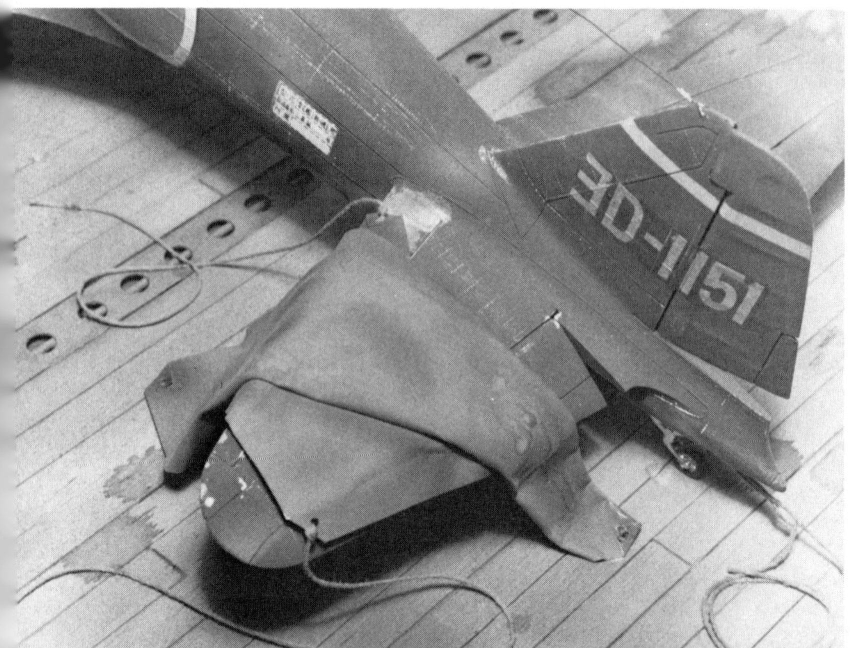

World War II-era aircraft look like the historical replicas they should be when resting on simulated concrete or tar pavement runways or, perhaps, surrounded by earthen bank revetments. You probably will not be able to resist the temptation to build at least one diorama depicting an aircraft that has crashed. The crash scene is the most difficult miniature scene of all to replicate faithfully.

Craft supply stores and picture-framing shops sell small wooden plaques that make perfect diorama bases for 1/72-scale single-engine aircraft miniatures. If you want to build a diorama larger than about 6x9 inches, I would suggest you purchase a picture frame of the size and shape needed for the diorama. A lumberyard (or perhaps the picture frame shop) can cut a piece of 1/8 inch plywood or cardboard to match the size of the opening in the *back* of the frame. The frame is then set face-down with the aircraft diorama assembled on what would be the back of the picture (see figure 11-2). Do not glue the 1/8 inch plywood or cardboard into the picture frame until you have completed the diorama. This method will allow you to stain or paint the picture frame to fit the decor of the room with no danger of any paint or stain reaching the diorama or the model.

The diorama for your aircraft can be large enough to include at least a portion of an aircraft hanger or the area surrounding the resting place for the aircraft. You can even make the diorama large enough to hold two or three 1/72-scale or smaller aircraft models. Most dioramas depict outdoor scenes, but I've seen one very realistic diorama that included two of the interior walls of the hanger (but no hanger roof) to create a scene of an aircraft being repaired inside a hanger.

Accessories

The details and accessories that might surround an aircraft at rest are available to match every popular miniature aircraft scale. The people, tools and accessories sold for N-scale trains will work well enough with 1/144-scale aircraft; HO-scale accessories can be used with either 1/100 or 1/72-scale aircraft although the people will be a bit short for 1/72-scale and a bit tall for 1/100-scale. There are dozens of soldiers and other detail parts molded in 1/72-scale for use with 1/72-scale tanks and other armored vehicle dioramas. Similar accessories are offered in 1/48 and 1/32-scale for use in military vehicle scenes.

Some of the figures and parts may require slight modifications to match World War I or modern aircraft but most of the changes can be completed by simply painting the figures in modern or early costumes. If, for example, you trim the helmets from World War II soldiers, they can be painted to represent shirt-sleeved World War I aircraft mechanics or uniformed ground personnel in a modern airport scene.

Figure 11-7. You can simulate a portion of an airport using 1/72-scale military vehicles and figures. This P-47D is a Testor's kit with facial tissue "tarps."

Landscaping

The shops that carry model railroad supplies will have almost everything you need to create any type of landscape. HO-scale trees are close enough to 1/72-scale to be used as-is. The steel wool material used for Architectural Scale Models, AHM and Bachmann tree kits can be adhered to small branches from real trees or bushes to make 1/48 or 1/32-scale trees. The leaves can be formed by using the green-colored ground foam rubber from these same firms. You can also form leaves using the tiny paper circles that banks punch from checks to cancel them. Dye them green in Rit thinned with alcohol. Spray the steel wool branches of the tree with a spray adhesive and dip the tree into the check cancellations.

Figure 11-8. Study photographs of full-size aircraft on their flight decks to find details for a miniature diorama. *Photo courtesy U.S. Air Force.*

Woodland Scenics ground foam and foliage material can also be used on real tree or bush branches for trees in a diorama. The ground foam in the finer sizes makes very realistic grass or weed textures.

Nothing looks more like dirt than real dirt sifted through a fine-mesh screen or flour sifter. Paint the base with white glue to hold the dirt, ground foam rubber or other ground texture in place. The diorama base should be prepainted beige or brown so the color shows through any areas where the ground foam or dirt does not completely cover.

Almost any type of plaster, including dental plaster and Plaster of Paris (sold in drugstores) or patching plaster (sold in hardware stores), can be used to mold hills or revetment mounds. Soak paper towels in a soupy mixture of plaster and water and drape the towels over hills or mounds shaped from wadded-up newspaper. Cover the newspaper with three or four layers of the paper towel and plaster mix. When the plaster has cured for a week, it can be painted and covered with the dirt or grass textures.

Simulated Runways

The smooth surface of a concrete runway can best be simulated by using a large plastic "For Rent" or "For Sale" sign cut to fit your diorama base. Scrub the back (the unprinted surface) of the sign with coarse-grit sandpaper, working in a circular motion, to duplicate the texture of concrete. Roughen the printed side of the plastic in a similar manner so it can be held in place with a resin-based glue like *Titebond*. Use a dull hobby knife to scribe lines representing the expansion joints between the concrete panels and, if you wish, to carve some cracks and potholes. Paint the joints and cracks with dark grey paint after the entire runway area has been painted to match concrete. Take a close look at concrete and mix

Figure 11-9 (right). The metal tree branches and the brown steel wool for this 1/72-scale tree are AMSI products.

Figure 11-10 (below). The AMSI steel wool branches were sprayed with Scotch Sprayment adhesive and the tree was dipped into check cancellations.

Figure 11-11 (opposite page, top). The check cancellations create individual leaves. The small bushes are lichen and the "grass" is green flocking; both are from a model railroad hobby shop.

Figure 11-12 (opposite page, bottom). The trees surrounding this P-61 "Black Widow" are model railroad products from Woodland Scenics with ground foam "leaves" and cast metal "tree trunks."

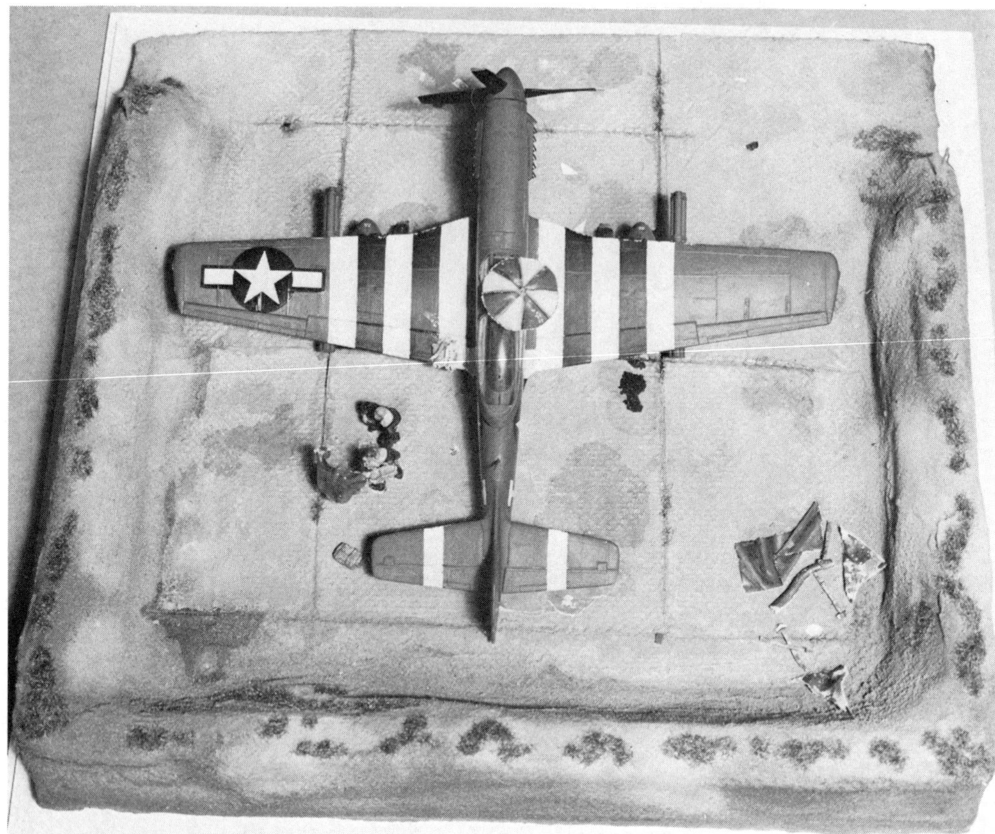

Figure 11-13. Many World War II fighters were kept in open air bunkers or revetments to confine any bomb explosions to just one aircraft. This 1/48-scale diorama was made from plaster-soaked paper towels.

a special batch of paint to simulate it. Most concrete is more beige than grey, with a touch of yellow. Weather the concrete surface with a spray-on "wash" of dark grey and black and apply a few oil spills with some dark brown or dark grey paint. For a super detail touch, glue some green flocking in the cracks to simulate grass or weeds. This same procedure can be used to simulate blacktop in 1/72-scale dioramas except, of course, that the surface would be painted a very dark grey.

For 1/48 or 1/32-scale dioramas, spread a 1/8 inch thick layer of plaster over the display board after the board has been sealed with several coats of paint. The plaster will be less likely to crack if you staple a scrap of wire screen over the surface of the diorama base and work the plaster into the screen. Smooth the plaster with lots of water and a leftover piece of plastic or metal sheet. When the plaster is dry, carve cracks and seams into the surface. Then paint it with the finer grade of non-slip decking paint or with indoor wall texture paint. Use whatever color paint you can

Figure 11-14. The runway for these three 1/72-scale Fokker D-VII models is a piece of grey cardboard stained with a piece of charcoal.

find; when it dries, cover it by spraying on a layer of dark grey paint. Accent the seams and weather the surface with dark brown paint applied with a rag. Finally, rub on some light grey paint to simulate the sun-bleached appearance of blacktop or tar-and-gravel paving.

Seascapes

The surface of the display base can also be detailed to simulate an ocean for seaplane, beach or crash dioramas. Build a completely watertight dam around the base with tape and aluminum foil. Mix enough boat-patching resin and catalyst to cover the board about 1/8 inch deep. Watch the resin carefully and, when it just begins to cure, push it into waves with a scrap of wood. The resin will go through a gelatin-like stage that lasts for several minutes before it hardens. A few drops of food coloring can be used to give the water a green, blue, or grey/green appearance. When the resin has set, touch the tops of the waves with Floquil's pearlescent Aqua-Cote paint to simulate whitecaps. Do not, however, pour the resin around any aircraft models: the heat from the curing process will melt the plastic. Form a mold around your model with aluminum foil and rest the foil in the resin while the resin is curing. The foil can then be peeled away and the aircraft rested in place. Clear enamel can be used to fill any gaps between the "water" and the aircraft.

Chapter 12

War Games

THERE is good news for those who would rather not relegate all of their miniature aircraft to a perpetual life on a shelf: the 1/72-scale and smaller aircraft can be used in simulated dogfights and other aerial war games. The war gaming hobby grew out of a game played in the early 1900s by shooting down toy lead soldiers with a cork-shooting cannon. Today's hobby is similar, in some respects, to the war games that are used by military commanders to simulate full-scale battles.

Simulations

The current selection of war games available from most hobby stores includes extremely accurate historical simulations. The war games, though, are simulations that take place primarily in the imagination of the players. The rules are designed to force each player to make the same decisions that the pilots and commanders made to determine the outcome of actual historical battles. There is no possible way of describing how realistic these games can be; you really have to play them to realize that the required level of participation really does demand almost the same decisions, with almost the same alternatives, as those that once faced military leaders. This same type of simulation is used, with equally effective results, in many of the games that simulate dogfights and other aerial warfare engagements throughout history.

One of the best-selling series of war games is published by Avalon Hill. Most of their games are based on battles from history including such epic struggles as the Civil War-era "Gettysburg" and the World War II-era "Panzer Blitz." The success of these games led to the development of Avalon Hill's "Luftwaffe", a game based on the dogfights during the closing stages of World War II. The Avalon Hill games are designed to be played with small cardboard counters to represent the aircraft and a playing board that represents the ground over which the aircraft fought their battles. A large number of aircraft modelers play "Luftwaffe" with plastic models of the aircraft that are represented by the cardboard playing pieces. The plastic models are only there to lend atmosphere to the game, however.

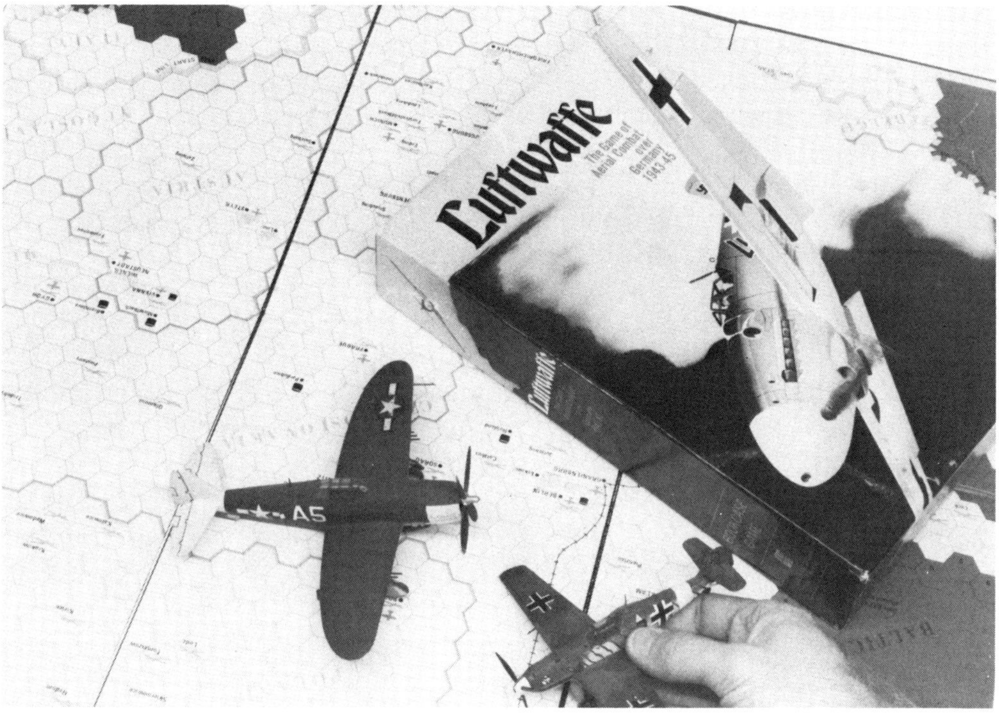

Figure 12-1. Avalon Hill's "Luftwaffe" game is played with small cardboard counters on boards with hexagonal spaces.

Avalon Hill's "Luftwaffe" is just one of a dozen games that simulate historical battles involving aircraft. Other games include different World War II battles as well as Korean, 1930-era and World War I battles. Lou Zocchi publishes "Battle of Britain" and "Flying Tigers," Eon Products publishes "Eagle Day," and Game Designers Workshop (GDW) publishes "Their Finest Hour," "Battle of Midway," and "Indian Ocean Adventure." These games are not designed to be played with plastic model aircraft but models of the appropriate aircraft can certainly lend a feeling of reality to the game. Some modelers develop their miniature aircraft collection to match the types of aircraft that appear in these hobby war games.

Three-Dimensional Dogfights

Anyone who has completed a model of a fighter aircraft has probably maneuvered it by hand through a simulated dogfight battle in the sky. Rocky Russo carried that fantasy one step closer to reality by developing a hobby war game that uses 1/72-scale fighter aircraft, rather than cardboard squares, as the playing pieces. The key to the game is a small stand on casters that holds a fighter aircraft model with a modified clothespin.

The stands allow the models to be maneuvered in *every* direction to simulate climbs, banks, rolls, loops and all the other evasive and attack maneuvers of an actual dogfight. Russo's first game to utilize the stands and 1/72 aircraft was "Mustangs and Messerschmitts," which deals with both air-to-air and air-to-ground battles and utilizes a choice of 137 different aircraft!

The list of battle games that can be played with 1/72-scale miniatures and the portable stands now includes "Triplane" (World War I), with "MIG Alley" (1950-era Korea and Suez battles) and "Legion Condor" (1920–1939 era) to follow from the publisher, McEwan Miniatures. The games include the list of materials for making the stands or you can purchase the stands through McEwan Miniatures.

These three-dimensional war games include a considerable amount of information about each aircraft that can be used in the game. The performance of each aircraft is rated against other aircraft of the period according to minimum speed, cruise speed, maximum speed, terminal speed, roll rate, climb rate, dive acceleration, guns, ammunition supply,

Figure 12-2. A 1/72-scale Fw 190A-8 attacks a Russian Lavochkin in McEwan Miniatures' "Mustangs and Messerschmitts" game. *Photo courtesy McEwan Miniatures.*

Figure 12-3. This clipped-wing spitfire is held to the playing stands with clothespin and wire but can still be maneuvered to simulate flight. *Photo courtesy McEwan Miniatures.*

service ceiling, when the aircraft saw active service, and other factors. The brands of 1/72-scale aircraft kits that replicate the planes used in the original battles are also listed. The aircrafts' performance tables are based, in most instances, on the actual flight manuals and performance tests of their era. The rule books include a bibliography listing sources of information on how the models should be painted and marked.

The games force each player to assume the role of the pilot. The players must use the strategy that is needed to win the battle as they "fly" into combat. The better war games like "Mustangs and Messerschmitts," "Triplane," "MIG Alley" and "Legion Condor" have very detailed rules. The aircrafts' mechanical performance is duplicated along with other factors that can affect the aerial battles including weather, morale and the pilot's ability (determined through an "ace system"). Instead of measuring distances according to the hexes on the playing board, players can use tape measures and reduced-scale distances. You cannot comprehend just how realistic your models can be until you strap yourself into the cockpit and take off for battle with an equally-realistic adversary.

Figure 12-4. The game "Mustangs and Messerschmitts" includes complete performance tables for 137 different World War II aircraft, including such unusual prototypes as the Westland "Whirlwind." *Photo courtesy McEwan Miniatures.*

Figure 12-5. A P-51D of the 352nd Fighter Group attacks a Messerschmitt Bf 109G6/R6 tropical in "Mustangs and Messerschmitts." Distances can be measured in inches or on the playing board. *Photo courtesy McEwan Miniatures.*

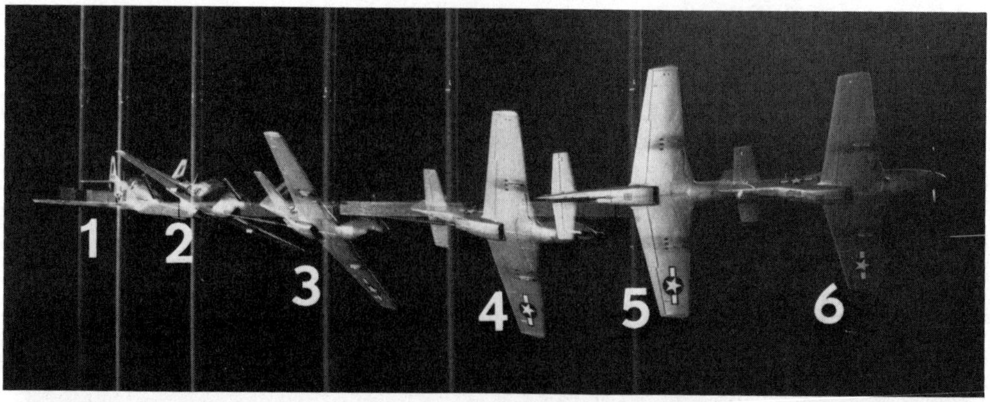
1
2
3
4
5
6

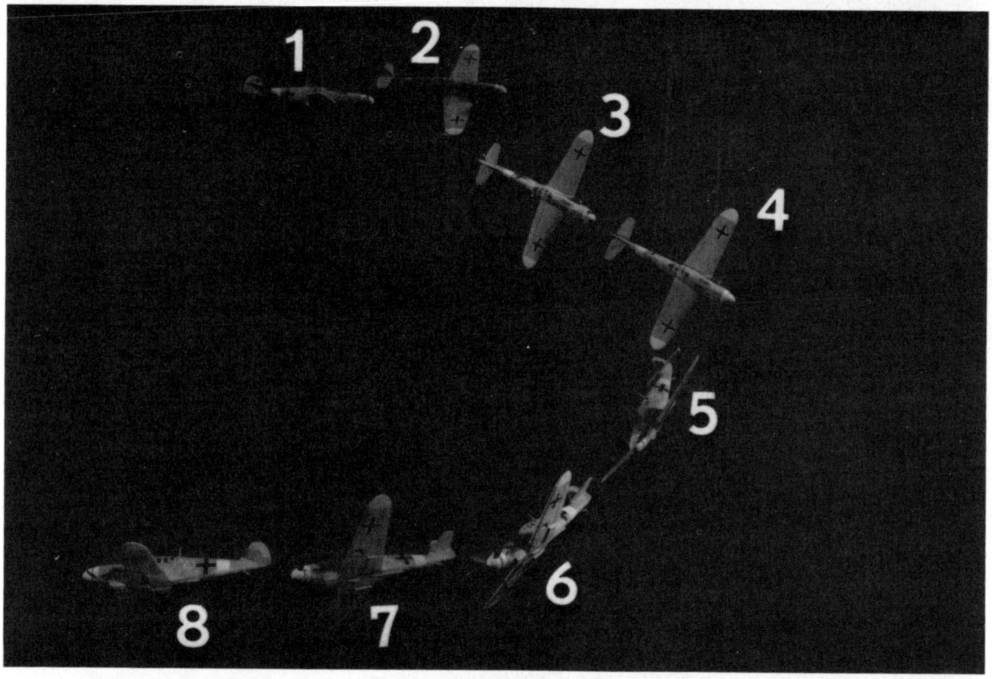
1
2
3
4
5
6
7
8

1
2
3
4
5
6
7
8
9
10

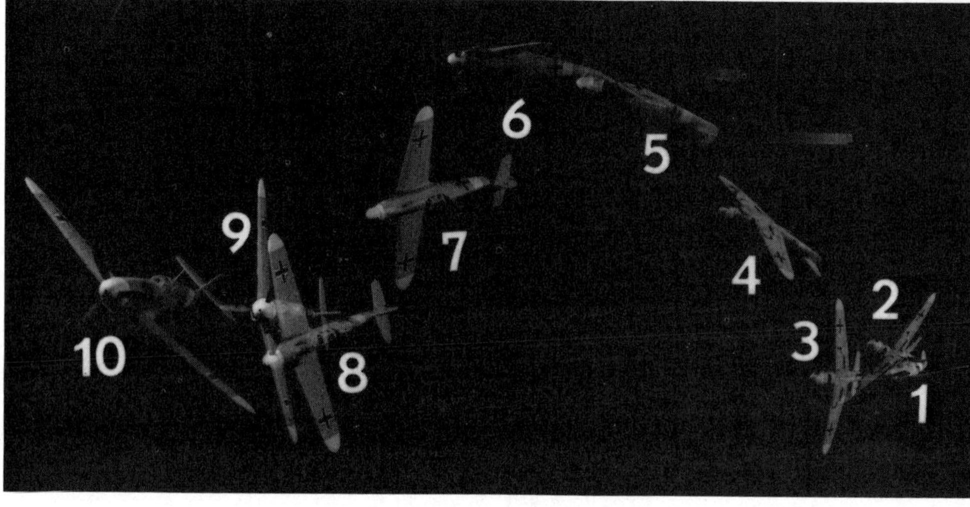

Figure 12-9. This Guards Lavochkin was painted accurately by using the sources of information included with the war game. *Photo courtesy McEwan Miniatures.*

Figure 12-6. The sequence of steps in the game for a P-51D Mustang to roll into a turn. *Photo courtesy McEwan Miniatures.*

Figure 12-7. Eight stages of an Me 109G-2 completing a "Split S" maneuver that could be part of a simulated dogfight. *Photo courtesy McEwan Miniatures.*

Figure 12-8. In the "Mustangs and Messerschmitts" game even complex maneuvers like this combat roll can be simulated. *Photo courtesy McEwan Miniatures.*

Sources of Supply and Publications

Sources of Supply

IF you write to one of the miniature aircraft product suppliers listed below to request the price of their catalog or other information, you must enclose a stamped, self-addressed envelope if you expect a reply. Some of these firms are part-time businesses operated by hobbyists, others are merely divisions of much larger corporations; in either case it may take some time for a reply to reach you. You can expect much better success if you can persuade your local hobby shop dealer to order whatever catalogs you need or to ask questions for you. You can locate most of the hobby shops in your area by looking in the Yellow Pages under the heading "Hobby & Model Construction Supplies—Retail." We have listed each firm's miniature aircraft supply specialty below its address.

ABT Decals
(See Polks)

Aeroform vacuum-formed models
(see Mail Call)

Airfix (USAirfix, Inc.)
P.O. Box 999
Hewitt, TX 76643
Plastic model kits

Airframe vacuum-formed models
(see Archers)

Airtec
128 South Road
Enfield, CT 06082
Jetliner model kits

Almark Decals
(see Polks)

AMT div. of Lesney Products Corp.
141 W. Commercial Ave.
Moonachie, NJ 07074
Plastic model kits

Archers Hobby World
18320 Ward St.
Fountain Valley, CA 93708
Mail order vacuum-formed kits

Architectural Model Supplies Miniatures
(AMSI)
P.O. Box 3497
San Rafael, CA 94902
Diorama landscaping materials

Associated Hobby Manufacturers, Inc.
(AHM)
401 E. Tioga St.
Philadelphia, PA 19134
Landscaping materials

Avalon Hill Game Co.
4517 Hartford Road
Baltimore, MD 21214
Hobby war games

Bachmann Brothers, Inc.
1400 E. Erie Ave.
Philadelphia, PA 19124

Bachmann Brothers, Inc. (cont.)
    Die-cast collector's planes and diorama landscaping materials

Badger Air Brush Co.
    9201 Gage Ave.
    Franklin Park, IL 60131
    Airbrushes and compressors

Bandai
    (see Entex)

Binks Manufacturing Co.
    9201 W. Belmont Ave.
    Franklin Park, IL 60131
    Airbrushes

Boyd Models
    1835 Whittier Blvd.
    Building No. B1
    Costa Mesa, CA 92627
    *Plastic figures
    (people)*

Brookhurst Hobbies
    12741 Brookhurst Way
    Garden Grove, CA 92640
    Mail-order dealer

Combat Models
    1633 Marconi Rd.
    Wall, NJ 07719
    Vacuum-formed kits

D & J Hobby & Crafts
    96 San Tomas Aquino Rd.
    Campbell, CA 95008
    Mail-order dealer

Dragon Models vacuum-formed kits
    (see Mail Call)

Dura-Tite filler putty
    (see Mail Call)

Entex Industries, Inc.
    1100 W. Walnut Ave.
    Compton, CA 90220
    Plastic kits

Eon Products
    96 Stockton St.
    Dorchester, MA 02124
    Hobby war games

ESCI plastic kits
    (see Scale Craft)

Evergreen Scale Models
    1717 N. E. 92nd St.
    Seattle, WA 98115
    Plastic sheet and strip material

Faller plastic kits
    (see Model Power)

Floquil-Polly S Corp.
    Route 30
    New Amsterdam, NY 12010
    Paints

Formicator vacuum-molding machine
    (see Idea Development)

Paul Freiler's Historical Models
    19510 Hawthorne Blvd.
    Torrance, CA 90503
    Mail order dealer

Fujimi plastic kits
    (see Scale Craft)

Game Designer's Workshop (GDW)
    203 North St.
    Normal, IL 61761
    Hobby war games

Gamescience
    01956 Pass Road
    Gulfport, MS 39501
    Hobby war games

Griffin vacuum-formed kits
    (see Mail Call)

Hasegawa plastic kits
    (see Minicraft)

Heller plastic kits
    (see Polks)

Idea Development, Inc.
    P.O. Box 7399
    Newark, DE 19711
    Vacuum-forming machine and plastic sheet

Italeri plastic kits
    (see Testors)

J & L Aircraft Miniatures vacuum-formed kits
    (see Mail Call)

Lesney Products Corp.
141 W. Commercial Ave.
Moonachie, NJ 07074
Plastic kits

Lindberg Products, Inc.
8050 N. Monticello Ave.
Skokie, IL 60076
Plastic kits

Liqu-A-Plate paints
(see Archers)

Mail Call Models
1525 W. MacArthur Blvd., No. 20
Costa Mesa, CA 92626
Mail-order dealer

Matchbox
(see Lesney)

McEwan Miniatures
840 W. 17th South
Salt Lake City, UT 84104
Hobby war games

Micro Scale
1821 E. Newport Circle
Santa Ana, CA 92705
Decals and glues

Minicraft Models, Inc.
1510 W. 228th St.
Torrance, CA 90501
Plastic kits

Mitsuwa plastic kits
(see Scale Craft)

Model Decals
(see Polks)

Model Power Corp.
200 Fifth Ave.
New York, NY 10010
Plastic kits

Model Rectifier Corp.
2500 Woodbridge Ave.
Edison, NJ 08817
Plastic kits

Monogram Models, Inc.
8601 Waukegan Rd.
Morton Grove, IL 60053
Plastic kits

MPC Division of Fundimensions
26750 23 Mile Rd.
Mount Clemens, MI 48045
Plastic kits

Munsell Color Corp., Inc.
2441 No. Calvert St.
Baltimore, MD 21218
Standard color chip guides

Nova vacuum-formed kits
(see Archers)

Otaki plastic kits
(see Scale Craft)

Paasche Airbrush Co.
1909 Diversey Parkway
Chicago, IL 60614
Airbrushes

Pactra Industries, Inc.
7060 Hollywood Blvd., Suite 101
Los Angeles, CA 90028
Paints

PanaVise Products, Inc.
2850 29th St.
Long Beach, CA 90806
Tools

Plastic and plastic kits
(see Polks)

Plastruct, Inc.
1020 So. Wallace Pl.
City of Industry, CA 91748
Plastic structural shapes and sheets

Polks Model-Craft Hobbies, Inc.
346 Bergen Ave.
Jersey City, NJ 07354
Mail-order dealer

Preiser figures
(see Boyd)

Revell, Inc.
4223 Glencoe Ave.
Venice, CA 90291
Plastic kits

Roskopf
(see Polks)

Scale Craft Models, Inc.
   8735 Shirley Ave.
   Northridge, CA 91324
     Plastic kits

Scale-Master decals
   (*see* Mail Call)

Spray-N-Plate paints
   (*see* Brookhurst or Mail Call)

Starplast plastic kits
   (*see* Polks)

Sutcliff vacuum-formed kits
   (*see* Archers)

Tamiya plastic kits
   (*see* Model Rectifier)

The Testor Corp.
   620 Buckbee St.
   Rockford, IL 61101
     Plastic kits, paint and cement

Thayer & Chandler
   442 No. Wells
   Chicago, IL 60610
     Airbrushes

Valley Plaza Hobbies
   12160 Hamlin St.
   North Hollywood, CA 91606
     Mail-order dealer

Waldron Model Products
   1358 Stephen Way
   San Jose, CA 95129
     Cockpit and detail parts

Weld-On cement
   (*see* Mail Call)

Williams Brothers, Inc.
   181 Pawnee St.
   San Marcos, CA 92069
     Plastic kits

X-Acto
   45-35 Van Dam St.
   Long Island City, NY 11101
     Airbrushes and tools

Publications
Magazines

Aeroplane Monthly
   IPC Transport Press Ltd.
   Dorset House
   Stamford St.
   London SE1 9LU England
     (Full-size aircraft)

Air Classics
   Challenge Publications, Inc.
   7950 Deering Ave.
   Canoga Park, CA 91304
     (Full-size aircraft monthly; also
     publishes *Air Combat*, full-size
     aircraft bimonthly)

Air Power
   Sentry Books, Inc.
   10718 White Oak Ave.
   Granada Hills, CA 91344
     (Full-size aircraft bimonthly; also
     publishes *Wings*, full-size aircraft
     bimonthly)

Air International
   Fine Scroll Limited (England)
   P.O. Box 353
   Whitestone, NY 11357
     (Full-size aircraft monthly)

Scale Modeler
   Challenge Publications, Inc.
   7950 Deering Ave.
   Canoga Park, CA 91344
     (Models, monthly)

Scale Models
   Model & Allied Publications Ltd. (England)
   % Bill Dean Books Ltd.
   166-41 Powells Cove Blvd.
   Whitestone, NY 11357
     (Models, monthly)

Book Publishers and Dealers

Aero Publishers, Inc.
   317 W. Aviation Rd.
   Fallbrook, CA 92028

Archive Books
   % Polks Model-Craft Hobbies, Inc.
   346 Bergen Ave.
   Jersey City, NJ 07304

Arco Publishing Co.
219 Park Ave. South
New York, NY 10003

S. Carwin & Sons, Ltd.
P.O. Box 147
Canoga Park, CA 91304

Bill Dean Books, Ltd.
166-41 Powells Cove Rd.
Whitestone, NY 11357

Grenadier Books
7950 Deering Ave.
Canoga Park, CA 91304

Historical Aviation
3850 Coronation Rd.
Eagan, MN 55122

Jeppesen Aviation Book Club
P.O. Box 2007
Latham, NY 12111

Kookaburra Technical Publications
214 Kenmark Rd.
Newark, DE 19713

Monogram Aviation Publications
625 Edgebrook Dr.
Boylston, MA 01505

Sentry Books, Inc.
P.O. Box 3324
Granada Hills, CA 91344

Squadron/Signal Publications, Inc.
1115 Crowley Dr.
Carrollton, TX 75006

Index